wales

Land of beauty and blessing

John Aaron and Gwyn Davies

DayOne

Series Editor: Brian H Edwards

DayOne

Using this book

We have focussed on places and people where there has been an evident work of God in the living faith of men and women, rather than mere formal Christianity. Many places and people have had to be omitted because of the size constraints of this series. Some important hymn-writers, for example, that would be of interest primarily to a Welsh-speaking readership, have been omitted.

Because some individuals are associated with more than one place – and *vice versa* – the index will help to keep locations and people together. In general, places are listed in alphabetical order for each county or region, although there are some exceptions where common sense dictates otherwise.

The counties that form the basis here are those that existed for over four centuries before the reorganization of local government in 1974 and 1996. Their boundaries do not necessarily correspond to those of counties bearing the same name today.

Many places included have their own websites. These should be consulted for accessibility, opening times and admission fees. Please respect the privacy of the many buildings referred to that are privately owned.

Detailed travel directions have been given. They are correct at the time of going to press, but circumstances may of course change. Post codes have been included for most locations as an aid to those with satellite navigation. For some sites the code will pinpoint a place within about fifty yards from the required location.

The authors

John Aaron grew up in Aberystwyth and followed a career in Welsh-medium schools, first as a physics teacher and then a school manager. He is married to Jenny; they have two children and five grandchildren. He has translated two Welsh books into English, namely *The Atonement Controversy* and *The Calvinistic Methodist Fathers of Wales*, both published by the Banner of Truth Trust.

Gwyn Davies is originally from Ynys-y-bwl, and was for many years a member of staff at the University of Aberystwyth and then at the Wales Evangelical School of Theology. He lives in Aberystwyth and is married to Glenys; they have three children and four grandchildren. His English-language publications include *Covenanting with God* (Evangelical Library of Wales, 1994) and *A Light in the Land: Christianity in Wales* 200-2000 (Bryntirion Press, 2002).

CONTENTS

© Day One Publications 2015   First printed 2015

A CIP record is held at The British Library   ISBN 978-1-84625-456-7

Published by Day One Publications Ryelands Road, Leominster, HR6 8NZ

☎ 01568 613 740 FAX 01568 611 473   email: sales@dayone.co.uk   www.dayone.co.uk   All rights reserved

Design: Steve Devane   Printed by Polskabook, UK

Welcome to Wales

Wales is a land of great beauty especially in its scenic coastline and stunning mountains. But it is also a land where the blessing of God has been known to a remarkable extent down the centuries

Even for the visitor, the evidence is there with innumerable churches and chapels, statues, memorials, and Celtic crosses. It is there also in place names. Those beginning with *Llan* – over 500 of them – refer to enclosed land on which a church was erected, often as long ago as the 6th century. *Llan* is usually followed by the name of the person who planted the church or perhaps to whom it was later dedicated. *Bangor* ('A church surrounded by a hedge'), *Betws* ('House of prayer'), *Capel* (Chapel), and *Eglwys* (Church) are also common elements in place names. Other places – such as the biblical names Bethesda, Bethlehem, Nazareth – come from the local chapel, reflecting the significance of the chapel at the heart of the community.

However, the influence of Christianity goes deeper still. Welsh became a distinct language during the 'Age of the Saints' in the 6th century, a time of spiritual revival in Wales. The 1588 Bible ensured its survival by providing standardized vocabulary and linguistic patterns, together with potent imagery for preachers and writers. From its origins in the 6th century, Welsh literature has been dominated by Christian writers and themes.

Time and again powerful spiritual movements have had a far-reaching effect on the social, cultural, and political life of the nation. Christians such as David, William Morgan, Griffith Jones, Howel Harris, Williams Pantycelyn, and Thomas Charles are regarded as among the most important figures in Welsh history.

This guide introduces a few of the people and places associated with the fascinating and often exciting impact of Christianity on Wales. It will also take you on an enthralling tour of a beautiful land where the reality and vitality of the Christian faith have been clearly and powerfully evident.

Facing page: A Celtic cross

1 North-west Wales
Majestic mountains, powerful preachers

In north-west Wales an impressive coastline and awe-inspiring mountains are responsible for a landscape of breath-taking beauty. In addition it has a rich Christian history, including the ministry of some of Wales' most powerful preachers

ANGLESEY/SIR FÔN

Llanbadrig

In an idyllic setting overlooking the north Anglesey coast, Llanbadrig (LL67 0LH) is the only Welsh church that claims a direct link to Patrick, the 5th century evangelist of Ireland. Tradition has it that Patrick, who may well have been a native of Wales, built the church to give thanks for his safe landing after his ship was wrecked on nearby Patrick's Island/*Ynys Badrig*. It has been rebuilt over the centuries, but if tradition is correct it stands as a witness to the early gospel links between the Celtic lands.

Travelling eastwards on the A5025, turn first left just after Cemaes for Llanbadrig; follow signs to the church.

Llangefni

The administrative centre of Anglesey, Llangefni has important links with two of Wales' most powerful preachers.

One was John Elias, who led the Calvinistic Methodists from Thomas Charles's death in 1814 to his own in 1841. He lived at Llanfechell 1799–1828, where his wife Elizabeth kept a shop to support him. In 1830, two years after Elizabeth's death, he married Ann, the widow of Sir John Bulkeley.

They lived at 'Fron', Llangefni. There is a small Welsh plaque on the front of the house (privately owned). A Welsh plaque inside the memorial chapel Capel Coffadwriaethol John Elias (LL77 7WY) erected in 1897 commemorates his ministry, characterized by a deep conviction of the divine origin and authority of the gospel, intense seriousness, and passionate fervour. His concern for biblical truth was expressed in his important

Facing page: Yr Wyddfa/The Snowdon range from Capel Curig, just after dawn on a winter's morning

contribution to the Calvinistic
Methodists' excellent *Confession
of Faith* (1823). As a testimony
to his influence, it was later
commented that, if a roof could be
placed over Anglesey, the island
would constitute an immense
Calvinistic Methodist chapel.

A bilingual memorial
marking Elias's grave stands in
St Catherine's churchyard, Llanfaes, Beaumaris (LL58 8LL).

*Above: Llanbadrig Church and
Patrick's Island*

*'Fron' is off Lôn Fron, a lane
on the left just before a low
railway bridge on the A5114 into
Llangefni. Moriah, the memorial
chapel, is on the right just beyond
the bridge. Llanfechell is off the*

A spiritual auction: an account of a sermon by John Elias

'I feel within myself
this minute to offer
[these drunkards] for
sale, by auction, to
whomsoever will take
them . . .' Then, with
his arm outstretched,
as if he held them
in the palm of his
hand, he shouted,
'Who will take them?
Who will take them?
Churchmen, will you
take them?' 'We? We
in our baptism have
professed to renounce
the devil and all his
works. No; *we* cannot
take them.' Then, after
a moment's silence,
'Independents, will *you*
take them?' 'What?
We? We, ages ago,
left the Church of
England because of

her corruption. No; *we*
will not take them.'
Another interval of
silence. 'Baptists, will
you take them?' 'We?
Certainly not! We
dip all our people in
water as a sign that
we take those who are
cleansed. No; we will
not have them.' Silence
again. 'Wesleyans, will
you take them?' 'What?
We? Good works is a
matter of life with us.
We do not want them.'
. . . 'Who will take
them? Who will take
them? Who will take
them?' . . . His eyes
flashed as he turned
his head aside, and in
a low tone . . . he said,
'Methinks I can hear
the devil at my elbow

saying, "Knock them
down to me! I will take
them." ' Then, after
thirty seconds of dead
silence, he cried, 'I was
going to say, Satan,
that you could have
them, but' – looking
upwards, he said in a
loud, clear, yet gentle
voice, 'I can hear
Jesus saying, "I will
take them! I will take
them! Unclean, to be
washed; drunkards, to
be sobered; in all their
filth and degradation,
I will take them, and
cleanse them in mine
own blood." '

A5025; the house and shop – now two houses – are on the corner of Rhes y Goron/Crown Terrace, in the village square. The graves of Elizabeth and other family members are at the far end of the churchyard, behind the church. For Elias's grave, pass Beaumaris Castle on the left, follow the B5109 for 1.6 miles (2.5 km), then turn left (sign: Llanfaes) along a lane for 0.5 miles (0.8 km). At a junction, turn left and then left again at the bottom of the hill. The memorial stands on the left of the gate.

While Elias was labouring among the Calvinistic Methodists, Christmas Evans (1766–1838) was actively promoting the Baptist cause on Anglesey. He had gone to north Wales in 1789 as an evangelist on the Llŷn peninsula, but from 1791–1826 lived in the house adjoining Cildwrn Chapel, Llangefni (LL77 7NN). His dramatic preaching, fuelled by his vivid imagination, resulted in many conversions and the building of numerous chapels. He sometimes gave too much rein to his dramatic gifts and lacked judgement in his doctrinal views, but his zeal for the gospel, arising from a 'heart swelling with love to God and man', is undeniable. Outside the chapel (rebuilt in the 1840s and now the home of Llangefni Welsh Evangelical Church) there is a Welsh plaque and also the grave of Catherine, his first wife. Penuel, a memorial chapel, was erected in the centre of Llangefni in 1897.

Cildwrn is on the right, on the road out of Llangefni towards Bodedern (B5109). Penuel stands at the junction of Stryd y Cae and Ffordd Glandŵr.

Menai Bridge/Porthaethwy
Church Island/*Ynys Tysilio* (LL59 5HD) provides fine views of the Menai Strait. A church was probably established here

Above: An imagined picture of John Elias preaching

Above: Cildwrn Chapel, Llangefni, centre of Christmas Evans' ministry in Anglesey

by Tysilio in the 7th century; the present building dates from the 14th or 15th century. Among the graves nearby is that of Henry Rees, the greatest Welsh preacher of the mid-19th century.

Having crossed Telford's majestic bridge to Anglesey (A5), go straight across at the roundabout (sign: Caergybi/Holyhead). Just beyond the roundabout there are small signs to Coed Cyrnol and Ynys Tysilio/Church Island. Turn left into the parking area and follow the tarmac path. For Henry Rees' grave (wording in Welsh), bear left after the gate at the end of the causeway, then right up a path with steps at its far end; the grave is on the left of the path.

Other picturesque 'island' churches include Llangwyfan (LL63 5YR; *signs from Aberffraw*), Llanddwyn (LL61 6SG; *signs from Newborough*), and Cybi's 'Holy Island' church (LL65 1HG) at – significantly – Holyhead. Puffin Island/*Ynys Seiriol* has ecclesiastical remains.

CAERNARFONSHIRE/SIR GAERNARFON

Bangor

The first church at Bangor, the main centre for north-west Wales, was established by Deiniol *c* AD 525–30. 'Bangor' refers to the fence of woven branches erected around the church. Much of the present cathedral (LL57 1RL), which may possibly have been erected on the site of Deiniol's church, dates from the 14th century. The Lady Chapel contains an English memorial plaque to Edmwnd Prys, a celebrated poet who helped to translate the Welsh Bible (1588) and composed a valuable collection of metrical psalms (*Salmau Cân*, 1621).

In the late 1940s and early 1950s there was a spiritual awakening among Welsh-speaking students at Bangor, including J. Elwyn Davies and R. Geraint Gruffydd, that led to the formation of the Evangelical Movement of Wales.

Next door to each other in Ffriddoedd Road (LL57 2EH), near the station, stand the Welsh Independents' Coleg Bala-Bangor and the Baptist College of North Wales/*Y Coleg Gwyn*, where many godly ministers received their training. R. Tudur Jones (1921–98) was principal of the former 1965–1988; a prolific author in Welsh, his English books include *The Great Reformation*. It is now closed, while the Baptist College is used for interdenominational ministerial training.

Above: Bardsey Island

Bardsey Island/Ynys Enlli

Lying just beyond the Llŷn peninsula, Bardsey (LL53 8DE) has a fascinating beauty and a wealth of wildlife. A church was probably first planted here in the 6th century by Cadfan, originally from Brittany, and there are ruins of a medieval abbey. The story that 20,000 saints are buried on the island seems to have originated in the Middle Ages, either through a copying error or as a basis for the supposition that three pilgrimages to Bardsey were equivalent to one to Rome! It remains a popular place of pilgrimage, not least among those attracted by vague conceptions of supposed Celtic spirituality. These unfounded traditions, however, should not detract from the fact that Bardsey has long and genuine Christian associations.

Bardsey can be reached by boat from Porth Meudwy, near Aberdaron, and sometimes from Pwllheli. There are glorious views of the island from Uwchmynydd, beyond Aberdaron.

Beddgelert

Visitors flock to Beddgelert not only because of its magnificent scenery but also to see the alleged grave ('bedd') of Gelert, the faithful hound wrongly killed by Prince Llywelyn the Great. The story, it must be said, is entirely fictitious. What is undeniable, however, is the powerful revival that began in August 1817 in a service at the nearby farmhouse of Hafod-y-llan (LL55 4NG) in the lovely Gwynant valley near the foot of Snowdon. The preacher, Richard Williams, was not renowned for any oratorical gifts but that evening, says one who was present, the Holy Spirit came upon him: 'although Richard Williams was speaking, yet somehow it was not Richard Williams . . . and the sermon was not his sermon!' The revival lasted until 1822; according to an observer, it was 'more general, more powerful, and more enduring in its effects than any previous one in north Wales', and overflowed into parts of south Wales too.

Take the A498 from Beddgelert towards Capel Curig. 2.5 miles (4 km) from Beddgelert, after a row of houses on the left and just before a lay-by on the right, there is a small low sign for Hafod-y-Llan in a wall on the left. The old farmhouse, now owned by the National Trust, stands beyond the present one.

Clynnog Fawr

In the centre of Clynnog Fawr, not far from the sea, stands the magnificent St Beuno's Church (LL54 5NG), dating from the 15th and 16th centuries. According to tradition, Beuno planted a church here c 630 – perhaps where St Beuno's Chapel stands, to the south-east of the church – but he also preached extensively in north Wales. The church contains a helpful historical exhibition.

Near the south wall a Welsh poem on the grave of Robert Roberts (1762–1802) declares that he spoke 'as a seraph from heaven'. Among those affected by his warm-hearted ministry and the reality of God's presence that accompanied it was Christmas Evans. A virtual cripple, Roberts nevertheless preached the gospel tirelessly throughout Wales and beyond. He also ministered to the Calvinistic Methodists at Capel Uchaf; the site is marked by a Welsh memorial stone, and offers extensive views.

Clynnog is on the A499 between Caernarfon and Pwllheli. For Capel Uchaf, follow the signs from the centre of Clynnog, via a steep and narrow lane, for about a mile (1.6 km). At the far end of the hamlet, as the lane starts to go downhill, the memorial stone is on the right, behind railings.

Dolwyddelan

The major castles of north Wales were built by the English king

Above: Tŷ Mawr, Wybrnant, birthplace of William Morgan

Right: An imagined portrait of
William Morgan

Edward I to enforce his conquest
of the Welsh, but Dolwyddelan
Castle was one of those erected
by Prince Llywelyn the Great to
protect his land.

The nearby house
'Tanycastell' – literally 'Under
the castle' – was the birthplace
of four brothers noted for
their 'eloquence, poetry,
music, theology', according to a
memorial pillar just off the main
road. The most eminent, later
known as 'John Jones Tal-y-sarn'
(1796–1857), is commemorated in
a Welsh plaque on the wall of the
house. He wrote the hymn-tunes
'Llanllyfni' and 'Tanycastell',
but was renowned especially
as an eloquent preacher. In
one important respect he was
responsible for a change of
emphasis among the Calvinistic
Methodists: his proper insistence
on sinners' responsibility to
believe in Christ brought a
healthy practical element to
contemporary preaching, but
at the expense – to some extent,
at least – of the divine origin
and application of the gospel.
He thereby set a precedent that
in later generations led to a
message more man-centred than
God-centred. He was buried at
Llanllyfni, near Caernarfon.

*Shortly after leaving Dolwyddelan
on the A470 in the direction of
Dolgellau/Blaenau Ffestiniog, the
castle is visible on the right. Just
before reaching the castle, pull
in on the left to see the pillar and
house. The obelisk marking John
Jones' grave is in the cemetery
behind the church at Llanllyfni,
near the boundary hedge,
surrounded by railings; it bears a
long Welsh inscription.*

Penmachno

St Tudclud's Church at
Penmachno contains a number
of very early Christian memorial
stones, dating from the 5th or
6th century. One bears a Chi-
Rho inscription – a symbol
comprising the first two letters of
the Greek word for Christ – used
by Christians from the early 4th
century onwards.

In a delightfully tranquil
setting among the secluded hills
beyond Penmachno stands

Above: St Beuno's Church, Clynnog Fawr

Tŷ Mawr, Wybrnant (LL25 0HJ), now a National Trust property. This was the birthplace of William Morgan (*c* 1545–1604), one of the most significant figures in Welsh history on account of his majestic translation of the Bible into Welsh (1588). An original copy is on display, together with some 200 Bibles in other languages.

Leave Betws-y-Coed on the A5 towards Corwen/Llangollen. After just over 1.5 miles (2.4 km), turn right (sign: Penmachno). At Penmachno follow signs for Tŷ Mawr, which is just over 2 miles (3.2 km) along a narrow road through the hills.

Y Ffôr
John Elias was born in the parish of Aber-erch on the beautiful Llŷn peninsula and as a boy attended the church there with his grandfather. His birthplace, Crymllwyn Bach (LL53 6NF) near Y Ffôr, has a Welsh plaque above the porch, declaring him simply

to be '*Pregethwr yr Efengyl*' (Preacher of the Gospel). It is possible that he was born in the older single-storey building next door, namely Brynllwyn Bach.

From Pwllheli take the A499 to Y Ffôr and turn left onto the B4354 (sign: Nefyn/Rhos Fawr). After a mile (1.6 km), turn right immediately beyond a timber yard (sign: Llwyndyrys) for a short distance. Crymllwyn Bach and Brynllwyn Bach stand together on the left.

MERIONETH/ MEIRIONNYDD

Bala/Y Bala
With its lovely lake nestling among the mountains, Bala is a most attractive town. Howel Harris was violently attacked here in 1741, but eventually – largely through the influence of Thomas Charles (1755–1814) – Bala became the centre of Calvinistic Methodism in north Wales.

A clergyman from Carmarthenshire, Charles settled here after marrying Sally Jones, daughter of a local shopkeeper. Rejected by various parishes because of his evangelicalism, he joined the Calvinistic Methodists, preached throughout north Wales, and energetically promoted schools – especially Sunday schools – to teach basic Christian truths to people of all ages. Through his magisterial *Geiriadur Ysgrythyrol* (Scriptural Dictionary), his catechism *Yr Hyfforddwr* (The Instructor), and other literary endeavours, he reached an even wider audience.

William Morgan and his Bible

It was probably as a student at Cambridge that William Morgan embraced the teachings of the Protestant Reformation. In 1578 he was appointed vicar of Llanrhaeadr-ym-Mochnant, on the borders of Denbighshire and Montgomeryshire and here, far from libraries and the company of scholars, he devoted himself to the daunting task of translating the whole Bible (published in 1588). He later became Bishop of Llandaff (1595) and of St Asaph (1601).

In the opinion of many scholars, nobody has had as much influence over Welsh life as William Morgan. By providing a standardized form of Welsh, his translation was to prove crucial to the survival of the spoken language and to supply a superb model for the written language. But his chief aim was to convey God's Word accurately and clearly to his fellow Welshmen. On the title-page of the 1588 Bible he placed a verse which sums up the basis of his life's great work: '. . . the holy Scriptures, which are able to make thee wise unto salvation, through faith which is in Christ Jesus' (2 Timothy 3:15). In the (translated) words of the poet, Siôn Tudur (c1522-1602),

'He brought to all men God's grace, Brought God's words clear to our face.'

Below: Title page of the Welsh Bible of 1588

After Williams Pantycelyn's death in 1791, Charles became leader of the Calvinistic Methodists, and, despite reservations, formed them into a separate denomination in 1811. His clear-headed scholarship, warm-hearted spirituality, and faithful dedication to the cause of Christ made him one of the makers of modern Wales. To many he is known as the man to whose house Mary Jones walked from Llanfihangel-y-Pennant to obtain a Bible, and whose response eventually led to the formation of the British and Foreign Bible Society in 1804.

There are plaques commemorating Charles and Mary Jones in Welsh and English on the shop where he lived in High Street, now occupied by Barclays Bank (LL23 7BH). A statue of Charles, erected in 1875, stands in front of Capel Tegid (LL23 7EL).

In the 19th century the Green at Bala (LL23 7NH) was the scene of Calvinistic Methodist association meetings, when vast crowds would experience remarkable spiritual blessing through the ministry of such preachers as John Elias and Henry Rees.

Outside the Calvinistic Methodists' former theological college stands an imposing statue of Lewis Edwards (1809–87), its founding principal (with David Charles). The college moved to its present site at Ffordd Ffrydan, on the A4212 towards Trawsfynydd/ Porthmadog, in 1863 (LL23 7RY). As 'Coleg y Bala', it now provides activities for children and young people under the auspices of the Presbyterian Church of Wales.

The Welsh Independents also had a theological academy at Bala, originally at the corner of Berwyn St. and Heol y Domen, opposite their chapel (LL23 7RR). It later moved to Bodiwan – on the left just beyond Coleg y Bala – and then to Bangor (Bala-Bangor College).

Bryn-y-groes, the Evangelical Movement of Wales's attractive conference centre, is at the Dolgellau end of Bala, near the lake (LL23 7YE).

Thomas Charles and Lewis Edwards – who married Charles' grand-daughter – are buried close together at Llanycil Church (LL23 7YF). 'Mary Jones World', a visitor and education centre, has been opened here by the Bible Society to illustrate the impact of the Bible on Wales and beyond.

For Capel Tegid, walk down Tegid St. (opposite the White Lion Hotel), and take the second turn on the left. The Green is on the right at the far end of Bala towards Corwen; a car park and fire station stand on part of the site. The original Coleg y Bala building, behind Thomas Charles' house, may be seen by taking about 30 paces along Plasey St. (off Tegid St.) and going through a pair of wooden doors on the right and then a pair of smaller wooden doors. It later moved to the building on the left by Capel Tegid. Llanycil is just outside Bala on the A494 to Dolgellau. The graves of Charles and Edwards are by the church wall looking towards Bala.

Llanegryn

Hugh Owen (1639–1700) – a relative of John Owen, perhaps the greatest British theologian – belonged to an influential gentry family. After studying at Oxford and serving as a teaching elder in the Puritan church at Wrexham, by 1672 he returned to his home at Bronclydwr, near Llanegryn,

Above: *Statue of Thomas Charles outside Capel Tegid, Bala*

Above: The Calvinistic Methodist Association meeting on the Green at Bala; John Elias was among the preachers

to nurture the Independent and open-communion Baptist congregations of Merioneth and Montgomeryshire during the persecution under Charles II. Through his preaching – often involving long and dangerous journeys – his distribution of Puritan books, and his pastoral sensitivity, he became known as 'the Apostle of Merioneth'. A memorial to him stands outside Ebenezer Independent Chapel, near Neuadd Egryn in the centre of the village. He is buried outside the Church of Saint Mary and Saint Egryn.

For the church, cross the bridge in the middle of Llanegryn, turn left up the steep hill, and take the second turn on the left. The grave is under a yew tree, almost in line with the church tower and some 35 paces away. For

Bronclydwr take the A493 from Llanegryn to Rhoslefain, and turn left for Tonfannau. After 0.5 miles (0.8 km), a private road, turning into a track, leads to the house. Please note that it is now a private dwelling.

Llanfihangel-y-Pennant
This remote hamlet in the foothills of Cader Idris is renowned as the birthplace of Mary Jones (1784–1872). The story of the 26-mile walk of this 16 year-old girl from Tŷ'n-y-ddôl cottage (LL36 9TU), now in ruins, to Bala to obtain a Bible from Thomas Charles, has sometimes been embellished and sentimentalized, but the core elements – including her poverty-stricken background – are undoubtedly true. The inspiring example of her earnest desire for a Bible was to be an important

Above: Memorial to Mary Jones at the site of her home, Llanfihangel-y-Pennant

factor in the formation of the British and Foreign Bible Society in 1804 to provide the Scriptures not only for Wales but also for the whole world.

Mary Jones was an 80-year-old blind widow when she died, but contributed regularly to the Bible Society to the end of her life. The wording on her grave at Bethlehem Calvinistic Methodist Chapel in Bryncrug (LL36 9PW) is in English, but around the grave are the words (in Welsh) of Isaiah 40:7: 'The grass withereth, the flower fadeth: but the word of our God shall stand for ever.'

From the middle of Abergynolwyn, take the narrow road for Llanegryn/Castell y Bere, and follow signs for Llanfihangel and Tŷ'n-y-Ddôl. Just beyond the impressive Welsh castle of Castell y Bere on the left, St Michael's Church has a

small exhibition in the vestry. Bear right after the church (sign: no through road). Just beyond a small bridge a bilingual memorial stands within the walls of her home (2.6 miles/4.2 km from Abergynolwyn). To follow her route, see www.maryjoneswalk.org.uk (Bible Society). For her grave, turn in the centre of Bryncrug (sign: Tal-y-llyn/Craig y Deryn). Bethlehem is on the right. Take the path round the chapel, and turn left up the slope; the grave is near the chapel wall and the top wall of the cemetery.

Maentwrog

Edmwnd Prys (1543/4–1623) assisted William Morgan in his task of translating the Bible into Welsh. A prolific poet, he is best known for his *Salmau Cân*, a metrical psalter published with the 1621 Welsh edition of the Book of Common Prayer. The only hymn-book used in Wales before the 18th century, these psalms were an important means of conveying biblical truths to a people who were only superficially acquainted with Scripture. Originally from Llanrwst, in 1576 Prys was appointed archdeacon of Merioneth, and from 1579 he settled at Tyddyn Du (LL41 4RB), near Maentwrog.

Tyddyn Du is usually associated with Maentwrog, but is nearer Gellilydan. Take the A487 from Penrhyndeudraeth towards Dolgellau, by-passing Maentwrog. Just beyond Gellilydan on the right, turn left (sign: Betws-y-Coed/Blaenau Ffestiniog). Tyddyn Du is the first house on the left, just beyond the turn.

A Welsh plaque at Cynfal Fawr (LL41 4RA), in the parish of Maentwrog, marks the birthplace of Morgan Llwyd, the Puritan preacher and writer usually associated with Wrexham.

From Llan Ffestiniog take the A470 towards Dolgellau. A mile (1.6 km) after passing under a railway bridge, following a number of bends there is a corner with a staggered crossroads sign. Turn right at this crossroads; after a short distance, turn right onto another narrow road. Cynfal Fawr is the first house on the left; a gate and narrow drive lead to the house. Please note that it is now a private dwelling.

Mallwyd

Tydecho probably founded a church here in the 6th century; parts of the present building – in the centre of Mallwyd (SY20 9AQ), slightly hidden from the A470 – date from the 14th century. On the wall is a Latin plaque to Dr John Davies (1567–1644), rector from 1604 onwards. The translation inside the porch speaks of him as '. . . A man of varied literary acquirements, An earnest defender of religion undefiled, Remarkably distinguished for the love of his country . . .'

One of the greatest of all Welsh scholars, he was mainly responsible for revising the language of the 1588 Welsh Bible for publication in 1620, and possibly also for the 1621 Welsh edition of the Book of Common Prayer. His grave lies in the floor opposite the plaque.

Tywyn

St Cadfan's Church (LL36 9DL), in the centre of the seaside town of Tywyn, contains some early Welsh Christian monuments. The 'Cadfan stone', a memorial stone cross from sometime between the 7th and 9th centuries, is the earliest example of an inscription in Welsh. Another pillar stone with an incised cross, from the same period, was used as a sundial to indicate the times of services.

Below: The 'Cadfan stone', St Cadfan's Church, Tywyn

❷ North-east Wales
'The Lord gave the word' – translators, preachers, commentators

North-east Wales is a fascinating amalgam of rural and industrial areas, coastal strip and upland moors, urban conurbations and attractive old towns — and the Welsh and English languages. It also has a special place in Welsh Christianity

DENBIGHSHIRE/SIR DDINBYCH

Corwen

Throughout Wales there are free-standing crosses, erected to indicate outdoor preaching sites. At Corwen an early example – probably from the 9th century – is now located at the Church of St Mael and St Sulien (LL21 0DL), round the corner from the church porch.

Denbigh/Dinbych

Three men named 'Thomas' dominate the modern religious history of Denbigh. First and foremost is Thomas Jones (1756–1820), the most accomplished of Welsh theologians. In the atonement controversies of the early 19th century he opposed the extreme views on either side and fought to ensure that the Calvinistic Methodists kept to a scriptural balance. Rejecting the Arminianism of Wesleyanism and the Hyper-Calvinism of others, he emphasized that Christ himself is the propitiation for sin (1 John 2:2); his sacrifice is therefore of infinite worth, sufficient for all, but effective only for those who trust in him.

Jones was a master of Welsh prose, as demonstrated in such works as his massive *Hanes Diwygwyr (a) Merthyron . . . Eglwys Loegr* (History of the Reformers (and) Martyrs. . . of the Church of England). His hymns combine biblical theology, fine poetry, and delight in the gospel; some – such as 'Mi wn fod fy Mhrynwr yn fyw' ('I know that my Redeemer lives') – are among the best in the Welsh language.

In 1811 Thomas Jones was one of the first to be ordained in the new denomination of Welsh Calvinistic Methodists. Despite ill health, he ministered faithfully

Facing page: Pistyll Rhaeadr, near Llanrhaeadr-ym-Mochnant, where William Morgan was vicar when he completed the translation of the Bible into Welsh (1588)

at what is now known as Capel Mawr (erected 1880), on the corner of Chapel Street/*Lôn Swan* and Beacons Hill (LL16 3ST). There is a Welsh plaque at 'Bryn Disgwylfa', the house he built a short distance down Beacons Hill, where he had a printing press for his books (LL16 3UD). His gravestone at St Marcella's Church/*Eglwys Wen* (LL16 4PY) states simply that he was a minister with the Calvinistic Methodists, a theologian, and a hymn-writer.

From the main roundabout leading to Rhuthun (A525), take the minor road towards Llandyrnog. St Marcella's Church is c 400 yards away, on the left. There is a modern Welsh headstone on Jones' grave, c 15-20 yards from that of Evan Pierce (the largest in the cemetery) towards Mynydd Clwyd.

Below: *Preaching cross, Corwen*

Also buried here in a well-marked grave is Thomas Edwards (1738–1810), 'Twm o'r Nant', famous for his 'interludes' which were satirical plays denouncing contemporary moral and social failings. His early work was vulgar and lewd, but through the influence of his wife and Thomas Charles some of his later plays were quite sympathetic towards the Methodists. A theatre and school in Denbigh are named after him. Mobs sometimes threw Methodists into the Lenten Pool/*Pwll Grawys*, now occupied by the roundabout near St Mary's Church.

The third Thomas is Thomas Gee (1815–98), one of Wales' foremost publishers. His father had been Thomas Jones' printer, and later bought the press. A prominent Calvinistic Methodist, the son developed it into a powerful organ for promoting Nonconformist values in religion, education, and politics. Among the large number of books published was *Y Gwyddoniadur Cymreig* (The Welsh Encyclopaedia) a ten-volume work presenting an impressive Christian perspective on history, geography, literature, science, etc. The press closed in 2001, but there are plans to establish a museum of printing there.

Gee's house (LL16 3AH) is on the right, towards the top of Vale Street, the hill into the town from the direction of St Asaph and Rhuthun. There are plaques on the wall and round the corner in Chapel St/Lôn Swan, where his old printing-works were located. For his grave, go back towards the main roundabout leading to Rhuthun (A525). After passing Denbigh High School on the right, turn right (sign: Prion/Saron). The cemetery is on the left; Gee's grave is marked by a tall column, but is simple in style and wording.

A board outside the Independents' Lôn Swan Chapel (LL16 3SR), in the lane between Gee's house and Capel Mawr, declares that the cause was founded as early as 1662 – the year of the 'Great Ejection' of dissenting clergy from the Church of England because of their refusal to be bound by what they regarded as the unbiblical dictates of the Act of Uniformity – although the first building on the present site was erected in 1742. There are plaques to Robert Everett, minister 1815–23 and subsequently a leading preacher among Welsh settlers in America, and to William Rees of Llansannan, minister 1837–43.

Above: *Thomas Jones of Denbigh*

Llanrhaeadr-ym-Mochnant
This remote parish, now in Powys, was historically divided between Denbighshire and Montgomeryshire, with the church in the former. Nearby is the spectacular Pistyll Rhaeadr waterfall, but the church (SY10 0JL), parts of which date from at least the 14th century, has its own attraction. William Morgan, who completed the translation of the Bible into Welsh in 1588, was vicar here 1578–1595. A commemorative lychgate, with memorial plaques in the adjacent walls, was erected in 1954. Inside, a hand-printed copy of his Bible, on loan from the National Library of Wales, is on display, as is the revised version of 1620. It is claimed that part of Morgan's pulpit may be incorporated in the present pulpit. Nearby Llys Morgan (SY10 0JZ), known as the Old Vicarage, is usually regarded as his home, although most of the building dates from the 18th and 19th centuries.

Two who subsequently held the living of Llanrhaeadr deserve mention. Oliver Thomas (c 1598–1652), a native of Montgomeryshire, wrote a number of Welsh Puritan books in which he described himself as *Carwr y Cymry* ('The One Who Loves the Welsh'). Charles Edwards (1628–91?), from Rhydycroesau, Llansilin, was the author of *Y Ffydd Ddi-ffuant* ('The Sincere Faith' 1667, 1671, 1677), a classic presentation of the history and truth of Christianity.

Llansannan

In the centre of Llansannan, high on the Denbighshire moors, is the bronze figure of a little girl beneath the names of five distinguished figures born locally (LL16 5HJ). Three deserve attention here:

William Salesbury (1520?–84?) was a noted scholar mainly responsible for translating the New Testament and the Book of Common Prayer into Welsh in 1567. Although marred by literary eccentricities, his work was of a remarkably high standard and provided the basis for William Morgan's translation of the whole Bible in 1588.

William Rees (1802–83) has a memorial chapel in his honour, erected in 1902 on the left as the A544 from Denbigh enters Llansannan (LL16 5HN). Better known by his bardic name 'Gwilym Hiraethog', he ministered among the Welsh Independents at Denbigh and then Liverpool. A prolific writer, he promoted numerous radical causes with the aim of making Christ's lordship over the whole of society a living reality. The English translation of his best-known hymn begins:

Here is love, vast as the ocean,
Loving-kindness as the flood,
When the Prince of Life, our
Ransom,
Shed for us His precious blood.

His brother, Henry Rees (1798–1869), is also commemorated by a memorial chapel, further along on the left. He too was a minister in Liverpool, but with the Calvinistic Methodists; after John Elias' death in 1841 he was regarded as one of the very best of their preachers. Indebted for his theology to John Owen and other Puritans, he was renowned for his godliness and the spiritual richness, warmth, and clarity of his preaching, to which he devoted himself more fully than his brother.

In front of this chapel is a Welsh memorial to Edward Parry (1723–86), a preacher, hymn-writer, and dedicated pioneer of Calvinistic Methodism locally.

Rhosllannerchrugog

Rhosllannerchrugog, often known simply as 'Rhos', is a former mining village with a strong Welsh community spirit, expressed especially in its rich musical tradition. It knew periods of spiritual revival in 1839–40 and 1859, primarily associated with 'Capel Mawr' (Jerusalem Calvinistic Methodist Chapel; LL14 2LA). It was also deeply affected by the 1904–05 revival, which began at Penuel Baptist Chapel (LL14 1BF) through the preaching of R B Jones from Porth – independently of Evan Roberts but at virtually the same time. One of those present recalled that Jones 'was a consuming fire and so was his message. And the preacher's fire consumed the congregation.' The

awareness of the overpowering presence of God spread to other chapels locally and had a long-term effect on the community.

From Johnstown take the B5426 for Rhos; at the first roundabout go straight ahead. Jerusalem is on the left just afterwards, at the junction with Osborne Street. At the next roundabout, take the road for Minera (sign: B5426). Penuel is on the left beyond the roundabout.

The Rhos area is also associated with William Williams of Wern (1781–1840). John Elias, Christmas Evans, and Williams were the three most powerful Welsh preachers of the period 1815–40. Although his theological views became gradually less sturdy, Williams combined the more doctrinal approach of the older Nonconformists with the spiritual warmth of the Methodists. He ministered among the Independents, mainly at Wern and Harwd, but also planted churches elsewhere, including Rhos and Llangollen; there is a plaque and small exhibition at Glanrafon Evangelical Church, Princess Street, near the centre of Llangollen (LL20 8RD). 'A preacher is not to be a *mountebank* entertaining people,' he declared, 'but the messenger of God in the matter of their souls.' When Wern Chapel was demolished, a Welsh plaque commemorating him was moved to Bethlehem vestry, Hall Street, Rhos (LL14 2LN).

Go through Rhos towards Minera. Bear left at the junction by the water tower; Williams lived in this area, known as Talwrn, for a time. Some 3 miles (4.8 km) from Rhos, the road stops climbing; immediately beyond a row of

houses on the left – Wern View/ Trem y Wern (LL14 4LS) – a memorial to Williams stands on the overgrown site of Wern Chapel graveyard. The road leads to Coed-poeth.

Rhos-on-Sea/Llandrillo-yn-Rhos

On the lower promenade at Rhos-on-Sea is the tiny St Trillo's Chapel (LL28 4RJ). Little is known of Trillo, but a number of churches in the area trace their origins to his pioneering labours. The original building was probably erected in the 6th century and made of wood and wattle. Although of later date and extensively renovated, the present structure still conveys something of the simple life of the Celtic saints as they took the gospel throughout Wales.

Wrexham/Wrecsam

Wrexham is the largest town in north Wales. One of its most impressive landmarks is St Giles Church (LL13 8LY), dating from the late 15th century, which has links with three important figures.

One is Walter Cradoc (1610?–59), a leading Welsh Puritan. A native of Monmouthshire, he lost his curacy in Cardiff on account of his Puritanism but then served as a curate in Wrexham, where his ministry *c* 1634–35 had a marked impact. Eventually a local brewer had him removed, but long afterwards Puritans, Nonconformists, and even early Methodists in north Wales were known as 'Cradocians'.

The second is Morgan Llwyd (1619–59), one of the best-known of the Welsh Puritans. Parliament appointed him as a travelling preacher in north Wales during the Civil War, and he made Wrexham his base. Probably by the late 1640s he was leader of the Independent church there which had its roots as far back as 1582, and made it the most important such congregation in north Wales. It may have met in a barn at the junction of Queen Street and Hope Street, on the site now occupied by Boots (opticians). As part of Cromwell's ecclesiastical settlement, Llwyd subsequently became minister at St Giles.

He was buried in the Dissenters' burial ground, now renamed as the Morgan Llwyd Memorial Park. The English words on the bilingual memorial stone state that he was 'the founder of Nonconformity in Wrexham'. A Welsh-medium school is named after him.

Morgan Llwyd

Morgan Llwyd was born at Cynfal Fawr in the parish of Maentwrog, Meirionnydd. Sent to school in Wrexham, he was converted there in 1635 through the preaching of Walter Cradoc. With Cradoc he was involved in the beginning of Welsh Nonconformity through the founding of the Independent congregation at Llanvaches, Monmouthshire, in 1639.

It was back at Wrexham, however, that Llwyd demonstrated his exceptional gifts as a preacher and writer.

A master of Welsh prose and poetry, his three most famous books – including the classic *Llyfr y Tri Aderyn* ('The Book of the Three Birds'), an allegorical work that explores contemporary political and religious questions together with the nature of true Christianity – were published in 1653. Because of his emphasis on spiritual experience and his attack on mere intellectual religion, he is sometimes considered a mystic or quasi-Quaker. At root, however, he was an orthodox Puritan who combined a deep-seated respect for the objective truth of Scripture with an awareness of the crucial importance of a living relationship with the God of the Bible.

Above: Memorial to Morgan Llwyd, Rhosddu Road, Wrexham

From the rear of King Street Bus Station, turn left along Rhosddu Road. Go straight across the roundabout towards Llay (B5425); the burial ground is on the right, a short distance beyond the roundabout.

Above: St Trillo's Chapel, Rhos-on-Sea

The Baptist cause at Wrexham traces its origins to the 1630s, probably as part of the above congregation, although its first chapel – 'The Old Meeting', in Chester Street – was built in 1762. The chapel has been demolished; Chester Street Baptist Church meets in the former schoolroom,

Above: St Giles Church, Wrexham

near the town centre (LL13 8BG).

In his early years Dr Daniel Williams (1643?–1716) almost certainly attended Llwyd's congregation. A prominent Nonconformist – although his theology was somewhat diluted – he left money to establish what is now known as Dr Williams's Library in London, a valuable research library of English Protestant Nonconformity.

The third figure associated with St Giles Church is Reginald Heber (1783–1826), who from 1823 was bishop of Calcutta, with responsibility for India, Sri Lanka, Australia, and parts of southern Africa. Among his hymns are 'Holy, holy, holy, Lord God almighty' and 'Brightest and best of the sons of the morning'. He married the vicar of Wrexham's daughter, and his fine missionary hymn 'From Greenland's icy mountains' was first sung at St Giles in 1819. The words are etched on a memorial window at the church, with a facsimile of the original manuscript on the window-sill. A plaque in Vicarage Hill states that it was composed in the old vicarage that stood nearby.

Vicarage Hill leads from Brook Street to the centre of town; the plaque is on the wall on the left-hand side up the hill, opposite a block of flats.

Outside the church's west door stands the tomb of Elihu Yale (1649–1721), a wealthy merchant whose family roots were in Plas yn Iâl, Llandegla, and who eventually settled in the Wrexham area. His business dealings were questionable, but he gave generous financial support to the fledgling Collegiate School of Connecticut in North America, whose aim was to promote Puritan teaching and practice. It adopted the name of Yale College and eventually became Yale University; a replica of St Giles' impressive tower stands on the campus. Jonathan Edwards, the renowned theologian and philosopher of Welsh descent, was both student and tutor at Yale College; David Brainerd (1718–47), the missionary to the Native Americans, also studied there.

FLINTSHIRE/SIR FFLINT

Bangor-on-Dee/Bangor Is-coed

Bangor-on-Dee is in Maelor Saesneg (English-speaking Maelor), separated from the rest of the old Flintshire by a wedge of Denbighshire. Known

Above: Original manuscript of Reginald Heber's missionary hymn: 'From Greenland's icy mountains'

today for its racecourse and impressive five-arched bridge, it is associated with a notorious event in Welsh history. According to the Venerable Bede, the army of Aethelfrith, king of Northumbria, slaughtered 1,200 of Bangor's monks after the Battle of Chester *c* 615. St Dunawd's Church (LL13 0AF) was probably built on the site of the monastery. No trace of the latter remains; the present church building dates from the 14th century.

Caerwys
Although usually associated with Denbigh, Thomas Jones (1756–1820) was born and spent most of his life at Plas Penucha, Caerwys (CH7 5BH). One of the most important Christians of his generation in Wales, he is described by a Welsh plaque as a scholar, theologian, historian, poet, preacher, and hymn-writer. Parts of the building date from at least the 16th century; the back of the house is particularly attractive.

Caerwys is off the A541 from Denbigh to Mold. After the welcome sign, bear left into Pen-y-Cefn Road. Continue beyond the last of the houses for half a mile (0.8 km) to a crossroads and turn left (sign: Sodom!); after nearly a mile (1.6 km) Plas Penucha is on the left.

Mold/Yr Wyddgrug
A busy little town, Mold was the home of Daniel Owen (1836–95), the tailor whose Welsh novels – e.g. *Rhys Lewis*, *Enoc Huws*, and *Gwen Tomos* – are essential reading for an understanding of the doctrinal debates and spiritual tensions of the period, although these elements are largely omitted from modern adaptations. A plaque on the wall of Y Pentan (CH7 1NY) in New Street, near the town centre, indicates the site of his tailor's shop. A statue stands in Daniel Owen Square (CH7 1DD), Earl Road, off High Street, while the nearby library and museum recreate his shop and study.

Owen attended Bethesda Calvinistic Methodist Chapel

(CH7 1NZ), a building with an impressive classical facade at the far end of New Street which contains a number of items associated with him. Outside stands a memorial to Roger Edwards (1811–86) who encouraged Owen in his writing. Edwards was himself an accomplished preacher, writer, and denominational statesman, although his rather broader theology and commitment to radical political liberalism represented a change from earlier Methodism.

Garmon, or Germanus (c 378–448), is celebrated in numerous place-names in north Wales and in the name of a Welsh-medium school at Mold. In 429, and perhaps again in 447, he came here from Auxerre in Gaul to combat Pelagianism, which challenged biblical teaching on the inherent sinfulness of human nature and the absolute necessity of the grace of God in the atoning death of Christ for salvation. He also secured a notable victory over pagan Pictish and Saxon raiders. An early account claimed that he ordered the native Britons to shout 'Alleluia' three times; the sound echoing from the surrounding hills convinced the enemy that they were facing a large army, and they fled in disarray. The 'battle' is commemorated by a monument bearing a Latin inscription in 'Maes Garmon' (Garmon's Field; CH7 5DA) in 1736.

From the A541 towards Denbigh, take the minor road towards Gwernaffield/Y Waun. Half a mile (0.8 km) from the last houses in Mold, there are large gates on the right leading to Plas Rhual/Rhual Dairy Farm. The column is in the – sometimes muddy – field opposite, near the boundary trees.

Below: Statue of Daniel Owen, Earl Road, Mold

St Asaph/Llanelwy

The original church here was founded c 560. The present cathedral (LL17 0RL) – reckoned to be the smallest in Britain and notable for its High Gothic architecture – dates mainly from the 13th century and is of particular interest regarding the translating of the Bible into Welsh. Outside there is a handsome Welsh-language monument to the translators: the 1567 New Testament is represented by William Salesbury, Richard Davies, and Thomas Huet; the 1588 Bible by William Morgan, Gabriel Goodman, and Edmwnd Prys; and the 1620 revision by John Davies and Richard Parry. Inside, in the Translators' Chapel, all three volumes are on display, together with the Welsh Book of Common Prayer and Prys' metrical psalter of 1621. Morgan, bishop here 1601–04, is buried in the cathedral; nothing marks the spot, but it is believed to be near the bishop's throne.

Above: Memorial to the translators of the Welsh Bible, outside St Asaph Cathedral

Trelawnyd

In 1701 the first Nonconformist church in Flintshire was established at Trelawnyd (formerly Newmarket). Matthew Henry, the famous Bible commentator, was the first minister; although living in Chester, he would travel to Trelawnyd on the monthly Communion Sunday. Now called Ebeneser or sometimes Capel Mawr (rebuilt in 1908), the church experienced revival in 1793 and again in 1905.

In the middle of Trelawnyd turn left off the A5151 from Rhuddlan into High Street, and then first right into Chapel Street.

Whitford/Chwitffordd

'Whitford', a pretty village near Holywell, is the name of a haunting hymn tune by J. Ambrose Lloyd, a native of Mold. Nearby stands Maen Achwyfan, a striking example of a decorated Christian wheel cross perhaps

dating from *c* AD 1000. An information board suggests that it may be a lamentation stone, commemorating an individual or a grievous event in the life of the community.

From the crossroads in Whitford, take the road past the church. At the first junction, take the road to Trelawnyd/Caerwys. 1.5 miles (2.4 km) from Whitford there is a road junction, behind which is the field containing the monument. Access is via a gate in the hedge, to the right of the junction.

Worthenbury, Broad Oak, Whitewell

In 1653 Judge John Puleston of Emral Hall appointed the Puritan Philip Henry (1631–96) as tutor to his children and preacher at

Matthew Henry and his commentary

Born at Broad Oak in 1662, Matthew Henry spent most of his life as a Presbyterian minister just over the border at Chester. However, he maintained links with Wales, serving also as minister of the Nonconformist church at Trelawnyd. A memorial obelisk stands on a roundabout opposite Chester Castle.

Henry is renowned the world over for his commentary on the Bible. The first part was published in 1708; he reached the end of the Acts of the Apostles before he died. Various Nonconformist ministers completed the work, partly from notes taken by Henry's congregation.

The commentary has been published over and over again, in both full and abbreviated versions. Its warm devotional spirit, simple explanation of the biblical text, and practical application of the meaning make it a spiritual feast for readers. C H Spurgeon described it as 'first among the mighty for general usefulness . . . most pious and pithy, sound and sensible, suggestive and sober, terse and trustworthy . . . suitable to everybody, instructive to all.'

Henry's comment on Genesis 2:22 is often quoted at weddings: 'The woman was made of a rib out of the side of Adam; not made out of his head to rule over him, not out of his feet to be trampled upon by him, but out of his side to be equal with him, under his arm to be protected, and near his heart to be beloved.'

Above: Matthew Henry

Below: Philip Henry

Worthenbury Church (LL13 0AW; rebuilt in the 1730s) in Maelor Saesneg (see Bangor-on-Dee).

Despite much spiritual fruit from his ministry, Henry was ejected from Worthenbury following the restoration of the monarchy in 1660 and suffered considerable persecution for his beliefs. He moved to Broad Oak, a property belonging to his wife, but because of his aversion to sectarianism continued to attend Anglican services, including those at St Mary's in nearby Whitewell/Iscoed (SY13 3AN). This attractive building, erected *c* 1830, retains roof timbers and oak panelling from Henry's time. In 1672 he was granted a licence to preach in his home at Broad Oak.

A Latin memorial to Philip Henry at St Alkmund's, Whitchurch (SY13 1LL), where he was buried, was later transferred to Whitewell; an

Above left: Maen Achwyfan, decorated Christian wheel-cross near Whitford

Above right: Whitewell Church, associated with Philip and Matthew Henry

English translation is provided underneath, and on a tablet at St Alkmund's. Known as 'Heavenly Henry', many of his perceptive observations were included in the well-known commentary on the Bible written by his son Matthew (1662–1714), who was born at Broad Oak and baptized at Whitewell.

On the right at the far end of Worthenbury, on the B5069 to Malpas, is the Old Rectory (LL13 0BJ), now a private house but built by the Pulestons for Philip Henry and his family. For Broad Oak, turn left (sign: Holly Bush) just after leaving Worthenbury on the road to Bangor. At a minor junction, turn right (sign: Holly Bush/Wrexham); on reaching the main road (A525), turn left for Whitchurch. After just over 6 miles (10 km) – almost 12 miles (19 km) from Wrexham – turn left (sign on the right: Whitewell; sign on the left: Broad Oak Farm Business Park). The house behind the business park (SY13 1LL) occupies the site of Henry's home from 1662 on. For Whitewell church, take the lane past the house, bear left through the village, turn right at the far end, and right again.

❸ Montgomeryshire/Sir Drefaldwyn
Forgotten heroes

Mwynder Maldwyn ('the gentleness or mellowness of Montgomeryshire') is a Welsh expression that refers primarily to the nature of the landscape. Some fine Welsh Christians have borne witness to their faith within this distinctive environment

Berriew/Aberriw

Not far from Berriew, a picturesque village just off the A483 between Newtown and Welshpool, is Pentre Llifior (SY21 8QJ), one of only two surviving 18th-century Wesleyan chapels in Wales. A simple construction using local brick, it was erected in 1798, although Wesleyan Methodism in the area dates from the 1760s, including a visit by John Wesley in 1769. 'The Preachers' Stable' opposite the chapel contains a small exhibition.

Thomas Olivers (1725–99) was probably among those who assisted the early congregation. Converted through the preaching of George Whitefield, he became one of Wesley's closest associates and was eventually buried in the same grave as Wesley himself. He was particularly useful to Wesley because he was able to preach in Welsh. Apart from the name of a lane there is nothing to mark his birth in Tregynon, a few miles west of Pentre Lleifior, but his heart-stirring hymn that first appeared in *The Gospel Magazine* in 1775 serves as a fitting memorial:

The God of Abraham praise,
Who reigns enthroned above;
Ancient of everlasting days,
And God of love;
Jehovah! Great I AM!
By earth and heaven confessed;
I bow and bless the sacred name
For ever blessed.

Pentre Llifior Chapel stands on the left, c 3 miles (4.8 km) from Berriew, on an unclassified road to Betws Cedewain. For Lôn Olivers/ Olivers Lane, go to the very end of Tregynon on the B4389 towards New Mills, turn left at the sign for Bwlch-y-ffridd, and then sharp right (SY16 3EH). The cottage where Olivers was born stood nearby.

Also near Berriew is Llifior Mill, Garthmyl (SY15 6SG). Thomas Jones (1810–49), son of the

---

Facing page: The attractive Gregynog Hall and Gardens (open to the public), near the birthplace of Thomas Olivers at Tregynon (see Berriew)

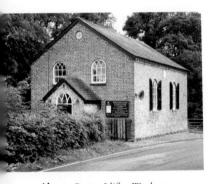

Above: Pentre Llifior Wesleyan Methodist Chapel

miller, became the first Welsh Calvinistic Methodist missionary when in 1841 he went to the Khasi Hills in north-east India. Here he pioneered the transcribing of the Khasi language and began the work of Bible translation. Others followed and eventually the gospel flourished there, not least through revival in 1904–06. There is nothing to commemorate Jones at the mill, but a bilingual memorial plaque stands outside Berriew Presbyterian Church at Refail (SY21 8QA).

Refail is 4 miles (6.4 km) from Welshpool on the A483 to Newtown; turn right on entering the village, immediately before the second sign for Berriew. For Llifior Mill, continue along the A483; half a mile beyond Garthmyl turn right (sign: Betws Cedewain), take the first turn right and then – by Brookfield House, just before the road begins to climb – turn left up a narrow track.

Kerry/Ceri
In 1649 the prominent Puritan Vavasor Powell settled at

Goetre, Kerry, as a base for itinerant preaching and pastoral care of the scattered Independent congregations of mid-Wales. Goetre (SY16 4NA) – now a working farm – became renowned for its hospitality and the important place given to household devotions.

From Kerry take the A489 for Churchstoke. After almost a mile, turn left onto the B4368 (sign:Abermule). Follow this road for 1.4 miles (2.2 km), then turn right. Follow a narrow lane for a mile, bearing left at a small grassy triangle and crossing a bridge over a stream before reaching Goetre on the right. (Note: there are at least two other farms named 'Goetre' in the vicinity.)

Llanbryn-mair
The 'Hen Gapel' ('Old Chapel') at Llanbryn-mair has an important place in Welsh Nonconformist history. The Welsh plaque on the building (SY19 7AG) states that it was first erected in 1739, but there was an Independent church here long before that. 'Eglwys Maldwyn' (the Montgomeryshire Church), with congregations originally containing both Paedobaptists and Baptists in various parts of the county, including Llanbryn-mair, probably dates from *c* 1650. The early ministry was mainly in the hands of Vavasor Powell and Henry Williams. After the restoration of the monarchy (1660) the church suffered persecution and congregations met in secret. When the 1689 Toleration Act provided freedom of worship, they

Above: 'Hen Gapel' ('Old Chapel' Welsh Independents), Llanbryn-mair

were nurtured by Hugh Owen of Bronclydwr, Merioneth.

At Llanbryn-mair a significant step was the arrival of Lewis Rees (1710–1800), a native of Glynneath, as minister in 1734. Under his lively preaching the church experienced spiritual revival and grew rapidly. Despite persecution, he preached throughout north Wales and brought Howel Harris to the north for the first time. He was followed in 1762 by Richard Tibbott (1719–98), a local man who had been an exhorter with the Calvinistic Methodists, and in 1778 and 1787 there were further periods of revival.

For much of the 19th century the church was associated with the Roberts family. John Roberts, appointed minister in 1798, took a prominent part in the atonement controversy of the early decades, arguing – in opposition to Thomas Jones of Denbigh – for a universal application of Christ's atonement. As the 19th century progressed, this attempt at 'moderating Calvinism' was to proceed far beyond the intentions of men like John Roberts. His son Samuel joined him as minister in 1827; known as 'S R', he was renowned as a promoter of peace and freedom movements, partly through his influential magazine *Y Cronicl*, but in so doing perhaps lost sight of the centrality of the gospel. Another son, also John but known as 'J R', became joint-minister with 'S R' in 1835. J R's theology, however, was a far cry from that of Rees and Tibbott, in that his Calvinism had become so moderated as to be practically non-existent. There is a Welsh memorial to the family in the graveyard.

Understanding Ann Griffiths and her hymns

The study of Ann Griffiths, especially her alleged 'mysticism', has become a growth industry in recent times. The key to understanding her, however, is to realize that she was a Calvinistic Methodist living at a time of vibrant revival. There is no doubt that she enjoyed profound spiritual experiences and had a passionate longing for a closer relationship with Jesus Christ, but these were firmly anchored in her clear and perceptive understanding of biblical doctrine and imagery. Here are two verses, translated by Alan Gaunt in *Hymns and Letters of Ann Griffiths* (London: Stainer & Bell, 1999):

Here we find the tent of meeting,
Here the blood that reconciles;
Here is refuge for the slayer,
Here the remedy that heals;
Here a place beside the Godhead
Here the sinner's nesting place,
Where, for ever, God's pure justice
Greets us with a smiling face.

Boldly, I will come before him;
His gold sceptre in his hand,
Points toward this favoured sinner:
Here, accepted, all can stand.
I'll press onward, shouting 'pardon',
Fall before my gracious Lord:
Mine the pardon, mine the cleansing,
Mine the bleaching in his blood.

Above: *Imagined bust of Ann Griffiths, Memorial Chapel, Dolanog*

From 1867 to 1881 there was a return to orthodoxy through the ministry of Owen Evans (1829–1920), a native of Pen-y-bont-fawr in northern Montgomeryshire and a relative of Ann Griffiths. The clear evangelical content of his books – for example on Christ's miracles and parables – led to him being called 'The Welsh J C Ryle'.

On entering the hamlet of Dôlfach, just beyond Llanbryn-mair on the A470 to Caersŵs, turn left (small sign on the right: Hen Gapel). Go up the hill, bearing left; the chapel is just beyond the railway bridge.

Two other important figures from Llanbryn-mair, associated with the Calvinistic Methodists rather than the Independent church, were the brothers William ('Gwilym Cyfeiliog' 1801–76) and Richard Williams (1802–42), descendants of Henry Williams of Ysgafell, Newtown, and nephews of the first John Roberts above. A noted poet, William, who moved to the nearby village of Bontdolgadfan, wrote the glorious 'Caed trefn i faddau pechod/Yn yr Iawn'. Here is the first verse as translated by Vernon Higham:

There is a path of pardon
In His blood;
There is a sure salvation
In His blood;
The law's full consummation,
A Father's approbation,
Hear Zion's acclamation!
In His blood;
Atonement and redemption
In His blood!

Bontdolgadfan is off the B4518
from Llanbryn-mair to Staylittle/
Penffordd-las, just beyond
Llanbryn-mair.

Above: *Owen Evans, minister at*
Llanbryn-mair, 1867–81

Richard Williams became a minister in Liverpool, and is best known for *Y Pregethwr a'r Gwrandawr* (The Preacher and the Listener; 1840), a powerful presentation of the sovereign purposes and actions of God in the salvation of sinners. His views, originally published in a series of articles and endorsed by John Elias, Henry Rees, and Lewis Edwards, drew an indignant response from his cousin 'J.R'.

Llanfihangel-yng-Ngwynfa

This pretty village in the northern Montgomeryshire hills is renowned as the birthplace of the hymn-writer, Ann Griffiths (1776–1805). Born at Dolwar Fach Farm (or Dolwar Fechan SY21 0NB), she was brought under conviction of sin at Llanfyllin *c* 1796, converted *c* 1797, and joined the Calvinistic Methodists at Pontrobert. In 1804 she married Thomas Griffiths of Meifod at Llanfihangel Church (SY22 5JH). The following year she gave birth to a daughter, but both she and the baby died shortly afterwards and were buried in the church graveyard.

Ann Griffiths received minimal schooling and spoke little English, but was part of a rich Welsh poetic tradition and had uncommon gifts for expressing spiritual truth vividly and powerfully. Her hymns were probably never intended for public use; rather, she would sing or recite them to her maid Ruth as a means of chronicling her own spiritual understanding and experience. Ruth memorized the hymns, and when she later married John Hughes of Pontrobert, he wrote them down and sent them to Thomas Charles, who published them in 1806.

Dolwar Fach is a working

Above: Ann Griffiths' grave, Llanfihangel-yng-Ngwynfa

Hughes and the providential way in which she preserved the hymns. The front porch wall contains the original Welsh words of the first half of the second verse quoted above.

An 'Ann Griffiths Walk' links places associated with her life. For more information: www.powystrails.org.uk.

Dolanog is on the B4382, off the A495 from Meifod towards Dolgellau. In the middle of the village, turn right to the Capel Coffadwriaethol (SY21 0LQ). Return to the B4382, turn right, and proceed for 1.1 miles (1.8 km) to Dolwar Fach (on the left; look for the white gateposts just off the road). From Dolwar Fach return to the B4382, turn left, and proceed for 2.1 miles (3.4 km). At Llanfihangel turn right for the church (sign: Village Centre/ Car park). A red granite pillar, with wording in Welsh, marks the grave on the left of the path to the church.

farm, but is accustomed to welcoming visitors. The present farmhouse was built after Ann Griffiths' death, but contains a room furnished as it would have been in her day. Llanfihangel Church contains a number of items relating to her, although at present it is closed to the public outside service times. In 1904 Capel Coffadwriaethol Ann Griffiths (Memorial Chapel) was opened at Dolanog; doors are usually unlocked during the day. Inside, there are imagined sculpted heads of Ann Griffiths, John Hughes, and two other local Methodists. In front of the pulpit stand two chairs belonging to Ann Griffiths; a Welsh plaque on the wall commemorates Ruth

Llanfihangel was also the birthplace of John Davies (1772–1855), a friend of Ann Griffiths who sailed for Tahiti in 1800 and spent the rest of his life there as a pioneer missionary. He prepared a dictionary and grammar of the language, and translated much of the Bible, together with the Westminster Assembly catechism and *Pilgrim's Progress*. Although he was blind for the last ten years of his life, he sent regular reports of the progress of the gospel to John Hughes. A simple Welsh plaque at the John Hughes Memorial Chapel, Pontrobert, commemorates him.

Above: *Dolwar Fach, Ann Griffiths' home*

Llanfyllin

The board outside Capel Pendref Independent Chapel in Llanfyllin (SY22 5BE) states in Welsh that the church was established *c* 1640. It is more likely that Eglwys Maldwyn (the Montgomeryshire Church), which included both Llanfyllin and Llanbryn-mair, came into existence around the middle of the century, but Llanfyllin was certainly among the early Nonconformist causes in Wales. Vavasor Powell, a leading Welsh Puritan, nurtured the congregation in its infancy. The first building was erected in 1708; destroyed by an anti-Nonconformist mob in 1715, it was rebuilt in 1717 and 1829.

Dr George Lewis was minister 1815–21. He had formerly been at Yr Hen Gapel (The Old Chapel), Llanuwchllyn, near Bala, but left for Wrexham in 1812 to combine ministerial duties with responsibility for the Dissenting Academy there. When he moved to Llanfyllin he brought the academy with him, and later took it to Newtown. He wrote an excellent commentary on the New Testament, while his *Drych Ysgrythyrol* (Scriptural Mirror) is among the most valuable volumes of systematic theology in Welsh.

The board also states that Ann Griffiths was converted here. However, it is probable that she was convicted of her sin at Llanfyllin but converted through her contact with the Methodists at Pontrobert. Moreover, the location may have been outside the Goat Inn, now the Cain Valley Hotel (SY22 5AH), in the centre of town where Benjamin Jones of Pwllheli was preaching at an open-air meeting arranged by the chapel. Her sister Jane lived at a shop opposite the hotel, now The Corner Shop/*Siop y Gornel*.

A plaque above the pulpit commemorates Susannah

The northern portion of the old Montgomeryshire is the main centre of the surviving – and growing – tradition of *plygain* carol-singing. Originally held early on Christmas morning – the word *plygain* is probably derived from the Latin phrase for 'before cock-crow' – services are now normally evening occasions in churches and chapels during the Christmas period. There is no set order: individuals or groups will simply get up, go to the front, and sing a Welsh carol, usually without accompaniment. It is a point of honour that they do not sing any carol already sung during the service.

Perhaps the most remarkable feature, however, is the carols themselves. Completely free from the empty sentimentality usually associated with the *genre*, they are rich in biblical theology and imagery, often celebrating the wonder and paradoxes of the incarnation in their proper context within the eternal plan of salvation. Here is a translation of the first and last verses of one of the most popular *plygain* carols:

*Today, when all was ready, as a babe,
as a babe,
Was born the root of Jesse, as a babe;
The mighty One from Bozrah,
The law-giver on Sina',
The atonement on Golgotha, as a babe,
as a babe,
Now suckled by Maria, as a babe.*

*Well hurry then, vile sinner, as you are,
as you are,
Seek refuge in the Saviour, as you are;
He'll wash you from transgression
White as the snows of Salmon,
And offer you his pardon, as you are,
as you are,
Come! Jesus bids you welcome, as you are.*

Rankin (1897–1989), née Ellis, a member of the congregation who from 1926 onwards undertook pioneering missionary work among the primitive peoples of Papua.

Pendref Chapel is at the Welshpool end of town, opposite the library/youth & community centre/sports centre.

Llanidloes

In the centre of Llanidloes stands an attractive half-timbered market hall (SY18 6EQ), dating from *c* 1600 and the only surviving building of its kind in Wales. At road level at its eastern end a stone states that John Wesley passed through the town at least six times and that, according to tradition, he stood on this stone to preach.

Llanidloes is also significant in the history of Calvinistic Methodism. At an association meeting here in 1750, tensions between Howel Harris and Daniel Rowland came to a head, largely because of the former's authoritarian personality, tendency to embrace some of the more dubious theological views of the Moravians, and readiness

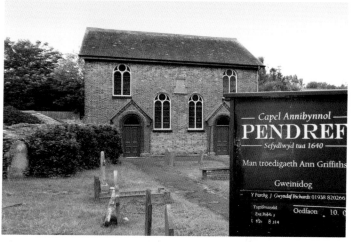

Above: Pendref Chapel (Welsh Independents), Llanfyllin

to accept the alleged 'prophecies' of Madam Griffith. As a result of their disagreement, the two leaders went their separate ways for several years, with Harris establishing a self-supporting community at Trefeca.

On the main road near the market hall stands China Street Calvinistic Methodist (Presbyterian) Chapel (SY18 6AB), built in the 1870s to replace a chapel in Bethel Street. In the outside porch a Welsh plaque commemorates Humphrey Gwalchmai (1788–1847), who pioneered settled pastoral ministry among the Calvinistic Methodists and contributed to their excellent *Confession of Faith* (1823). In 1953 Bobi Jones was converted here; subsequently Professor of Welsh at Aberystwyth University, he has contended earnestly for biblical Christianity and its application to every sphere of life.

Just beyond the chapel, on the corner of Mount Street opposite the Mount Inn, a plaque on Perllandy (now Orchard House; SY18 6EZ) states that the building may date from the early 16th century and that it was used as an early Baptist meeting-place.

Although the house is no longer standing, Mount Street was the birthplace of John Mills (1812–73), an accomplished musician who became a Calvinistic Methodist minister and, in 1846, an evangelist among the Jews of London.

Machynlleth

Machynlleth has a rich history, including Owain Glyndŵr's parliament here in 1404, but at times it has shown decided opposition to the gospel. Howel Harris was violently assaulted and shot at here in 1740, and a mob attacked Ioan Thomas in 1753. More recently, it has become

Above: *Market hall, Llanidloes. John Wesley preached from the stone at the bottom right-hand corner of the building*

associated with the 'New Age' movement.

It deserves mention, however, if only for the grave of the missionary David Griffiths (1792–1863) outside the Welsh Independents' Capel y Graig (1789) – a good example of early Nonconformist architecture. The inscription declares that Griffiths, who died here in 1863, 'laboured incessantly in the translation and revision of Scripture and other books to hasten the evangelization of Madagascar, which throughout was the great object of his life.'

Just beyond Tabernacle Museum of Modern Art on Heol Penrallt, an alleyway leads to Capel y Graig (SY20 8AR). Griffiths' grave is the only box grave there.

Montgomery/Trefaldwyn

George Herbert (1593–1633) was born in Montgomery, possibly in the famous castle but more likely at his family's town residence, Black Hall, which is no longer standing. He was briefly MP for Montgomery but then became a humble clergyman at Bemerton, Salisbury. Through *The Temple*, his volume of poetry, he has become one of the best-loved of Christian poets. The Puritan Richard Baxter wrote of him: 'Herbert speaks to God like one that really believeth a God, and whose business in the world is most with God. Heart-work and heaven-work make up his books.' Some of his poems have been turned into memorable hymns, including 'Let all the world in every corner sing', 'King of glory,

King of peace', and 'Teach me, my God and King'.

The ornate tomb of Herbert's parents, Sir Richard Herbert, Lord of Cherbury, and his wife Magdalen, is in the Norman church of St Nicholas (SY15 6PX). Magdalen Herbert was a patron and friend of John Donne (1572–1631), who claimed descent from the Dwnn family of Kidwelly. It is noteworthy that three of the best-known English metaphysical poets – Herbert, Donne and Henry Vaughan – were Welsh or of Welsh stock.

New Mills/Felin Newydd

An English plaque on a house at the village of New Mills (SY16 3NH) indicates the birthplace of John Pugh (1846–1907), founder of the Welsh Calvinistic Methodist Forward Movement. For 20 years as a minister he devoted himself to evangelistic preaching in the industrial towns of south Wales. Then, in 1891, he began a work among the English-speaking workers of Splott in Cardiff that led to the formation of the Forward Movement as a means of reaching those increasingly estranged from more formal religious provision. Pugh sought co-workers with 'grace, grit, and gumption' to take up the challenge, and their efforts met with considerable success.

New Mills is on the B4389 from Newtown to Llanfair Caereinion. The house is part of a short row on the right on the road to Berriew, just beyond the turn to Llanfair Caereinion.

The work was generously supported by another Montgomeryshire man, namely Edward Davies, son of the famous industrialist (and Calvinistic

Above: *Tomb of George Herbert's parents, St Nicholas's Church, Montgomery*

Above: John Pugh

Top: George Herbert

Newtown/Y Drenewydd

The largest town in Powys, Newtown was a 'new town' as long ago as the 13th century! Nearby is 'Ysgafell', the home of Henry Williams (1624–84), a godly and indefatigable Puritan preacher probably converted through Vavasor Powell's ministry. With other Nonconformists, he and his family suffered cruel persecution after the restoration of the monarchy in 1660. He was beaten and imprisoned, his father was killed, and his wife and children on one occasion had to flee across the river Severn for safety. Tradition has it that, after his property and goods had been plundered and burnt, a field sown with wheat produced a remarkable crop, more than sufficient to support his family and make up his losses. This field became known far and wide as 'Cae'r Fendith' (The Field of Blessing).

Parts of 'Ysgafell', now called 'Clarinor Manor', have been modernized. 'Cae'r Fendith' is adjacent to 'Middle Scafell' (SY16 3HQ), the house to the left; now bisected by the B4568, it runs down to the river. Further information may be obtained from 'Middle Scafell'.

From Broad Street in the centre of Newtown, go over the Long Bridge, and at the roundabout turn left into Milford Road for Aberhafesb (B4568). After 1.5 miles (2.4 km), turn right by a small sign for 'Middle Scafell', on the right, almost at road level. 'Ysgafell' is on the right among the buildings above the road.

Methodist) David Davies. There are impressive statues of the latter at the roadside in Llandinam, his home village (between Llanidloes and Newtown; SY17 5DG), and outside the Barry Dock Offices. Edward Davies lived at Plas Dinam, a country house near Llandinam which now offers holidays and incorporates a small museum. His daughters, Gwendoline and Margaret, later bought Gregynog Hall, located in a magnificent setting near Tregynon (open to the public).

Above: John Hughes Memorial Chapel, Pontrobert

Pontrobert

What is now known as the John Hughes Memorial Chapel, Pontrobert (SY22 6JT), was built in 1800. Similar to many rural buildings, its simple structure is a good example of early Welsh chapels. In the beginning it also housed a school, with John Hughes (1775–1854), a local weaver, as one of the teachers. Following his ordination with the Calvinistic Methodists in 1814, he ministered at the chapel and lived in the adjacent cottage. A hatch – still to be seen – was opened between the cottage and chapel to enable him to preach to the congregation from his sickbed. An important hymn-writer himself, he was also a source of spiritual instruction and encouragement to Ann Griffiths and wrote down her hymns, recounted from memory by his wife Ruth, her former maid.

Now sympathetically restored, the building houses the Centre for Christian Unity and Renewal and contains numerous items of interest. There is a delightful Welsh tribute to John Hughes and his wife on the memorial stone in the graveyard opposite.

About 2 miles (3.2 km) from Meifod on the A495 to Dolgellau, turn right (sign: Pontrobert). At the junction opposite the church, turn right. Just beyond the road to Llanfihangel on the left, turn left onto a no through road (signs: Hen Gapel John Hughes/Llwybr Ann Griffiths) for a short distance and turn into the parking ground in front of the chapel.

➍ Brecon and Radnor
Christ's sheep, Christ's shepherds

These two ancient counties reputedly have more sheep than people, but the beautiful Brecon Beacons National Park and the grassy hills and deep-cut valleys of Radnorshire have a particular charm

Brecon/Aberhonddu

Brecon is an attractive town with handsome Georgian buildings. One of its most remarkable sons, who served as mayor in 1772, is Thomas Coke (1747–1814). He was converted through reading Joseph Alleine's *An Alarm to the Unconverted*, and served as a curate at South Petherton, Somerset. Expelled from his curacy because of his 'Methodism' – a Coke Memorial Methodist Church was erected at South Petherton in 1882 – he became an itinerant preacher and secretary to John Wesley. On Wesley's death in 1791, Coke was appointed secretary of the Methodist Conference.

He is best known, however, as 'the Father of Methodist Missions', undertaking missionary journeys to Europe and beyond, including numerous visits to America and the West Indies. Appointed superintendent of all Wesleyan work in America in 1784, he and Francis Asbury established the Methodist Episcopal Church there. In 1813 he set sail at his own expense for the East Indies, but died at sea. According to Asbury, he was 'as a minister of Christ, in zeal, in labours, in services, the greatest man in the last century.'

His birthplace is marked by plaques on the building opposite the Guildhall in High Street, and at the back of a building in Church Lane. There are also memorial plaques at the foot of the outside wall of St Mary's Church nearby (LD3 7DJ), and between the porch and St Keyne's Chapel in Brecon Cathedral (LD3 9DP).

The cathedral, originally a Benedictine priory founded in 1093 perhaps on the site of a Celtic church, contains a heritage centre. A number of Brecon chapels are also of interest. The original building of the Plough Chapel (LD3 7AW) in Lion Street dates from 1699. 'Huntingdon House' (LD3 7NB) in the street

Facing page: Llyn Syfaddan/Llangorse Lake, near Trefeca, home of Howel Harris

Above: Thomas Coke

opposite the road leading to the cathedral, was initially erected in 1780 for the Calvinistic Methodists by the Countess of Huntingdon, the English aristocrat prominent in the 18th century evangelical revival.

In the 1860s the Welsh Independents opened their Memorial College in place of the old Dissenting Academy which had been transferred to Brecon in 1839. Their aim was to commemorate the official beginning of Nonconformity as a result of the 'Great Ejection' of 1662, when large numbers of clergy were obliged to leave the Anglican Church because of their opposition to the demands of the Act of Uniformity. The building is now divided into flats (Camden Court; LD3 7RP).

Capel-y-ffin

The unclassified road from Hay to Capel-y-ffin offers glorious views as it climbs to the Gospel Pass. Although no firm evidence exists, this name may reflect the influence of the Lollards, the followers of John Wycliffe (c 1330–84), who sought refuge and received support in the secluded valleys nearby. Walter Brut (c 1390–1402), the Lollard who described himself as 'sinner, layman, farmer, Christian, descended from the Welsh through both parents', was probably from this border country.

Some believe that Sir John Oldcastle (executed 1417) – a Lollard who turned to armed rebellion against Henry V, and was in part the model for Shakespeare's Falstaff – was eventually captured in this area. The village of Oldcastle, part of his family estate, lies between Llanthony/*Llanddewi Nant Hodni* and Llanvihangel Crucorney/*Llanfihangel Crucornau*.

It has been claimed that there were Baptists as early as 1633 in the neighbouring Olchon valley – in Herefordshire, but partly within the diocese of St David's, and largely Welsh-speaking then. However, the first reliable reference to Baptists in Olchon speaks of their participation in the Baptist cause at Hay in 1650. A branch of this church met at Capel-y-ffin in the 1730s, and a building was erected in 1762 (NP7 7NP) – the first and only Baptist chapel in close proximity to Olchon. There is a plaque on the chapel wall. (The nearby farm's postcode is NP7 7NP, but instead of turning right into the farm continue for a short distance along the road to the chapel.)

The name 'Capel-y-ffin' refers

Above: Llanlleonfel Church, where Charles Wesley married Sarah Gwynne

to the church, one of the smallest in Wales, and described by the diarist Francis Kilvert as looking like 'a stout grey owl'.

Garth

A lane leads from the centre of Garth to Garth House (LD4 4AL; in private ownership). In 1737 Marmaduke Gwynne (1694?–1769) set out from here as a magistrate to put a stop to Howel Harris's preaching in nearby Llangamarch. In the event, he was converted through a sermon by Harris and became one of the first members of the gentry to demonstrate public support for the Methodists. Gwynne also welcomed Whitefield and the Wesleys to Garth House. One tradition has it that Charles Wesley, seeing a small bird seeking shelter from a storm outside, was here inspired to write the hymn

'Jesu, Lover of my soul', including the words 'Hide me, O my Saviour, hide, Till the storm of life be past'.

At the nearby church of

Llanlleonfel/*Llanllywenfel* (LD4 4AW) John Wesley in 1749 conducted the wedding of Charles and Sarah, Gwynne's daughter. The church (rebuilt 1876) has a modern plaque commemorating the occasion, memorial tablets to the Gwynnes, and a striking stained-glass window containing the words 'Thou of life the fountain art' from the above hymn.

Take the A483 from Garth towards Beulah. 0.8 miles (1.3 km) from Garth, shortly after a rough lay-by on the left and just beyond a sign indicating a road going off to the right, turn left suddenly up a narrow track for a short distance. There is a small wooden sign on the roadside opposite the track, but it is difficult to see. The church stands among trees and is not visible from the road.

Hay-on-Wye/Y Gelli Gandryll

Renowned as 'the town of books' and the home of a popular festival of literature and the arts, Hay also has a claim to fame – and infamy – in Welsh Christianity.

Wedding day at Llanlleonfel

There is something quite remarkable about the wedding in 1749 of Sarah Gwynne, a member of a fairly minor gentry family, to Charles Wesley, perhaps the greatest hymn-writer in the English language. The ceremony was conducted by none other than John, Charles' brother and one of the greatest preachers of the 18th century. It was held in a simple little building in the heart of the Welsh countryside, with some eight other people present.

This is how John Wesley described the occasion: 'I married my brother and Sarah Gwynne. It was a solemn day, such as became the dignity of a Christian marriage.' Charles was rather more effusive: 'Not a cloud was to be seen from morning to night. I rose at four; spent three hours and a half in prayer or singing with my brother, with Sally [Sarah], with Beck. At eight I led Sally to church... We walked back to the house and joined again in prayer. Prayer and thanksgiving was our whole employment. We were cheerful without mirth, serious without sadness . . . My brother seemed the happiest person among us.'

The marriage was to be particularly happy.

Through Vavasor Powell and Walter Cradoc, a congregation containing both Baptists and Paedobaptists was established at nearby Llanigon at an early date, probably in the 1640s. Under John Miles' influence, a group from here in 1650 founded a Baptist church at Hay, drawing members from a wide area. Salem Baptist Chapel (HR3 5AG) was erected at Bell Bank/Oxford Terrace, at the top of the Bull Ring, c 1814 (rebuilt 1878), but the adjoining schoolroom is much older. A plaque on the schoolroom wall states that this is the second oldest Nonconformist chapel in Wales, and that the building dates from 1647. There is no firm evidence for these claims, but the historical significance of the Hay Baptist congregation is undeniable.

A steep lane next to the Old Black Lion in Lion Street leads to the Green (HR3 5AD), an

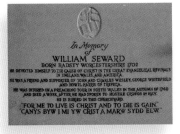

Above: Memorial plaque to William Seward, St Mary's Church, Cusop

open piece of land by the Dulas Brook. In October 1740 Howel Harris and William Seward were preaching here when somebody in the mob threw a stone that knocked Seward unconscious. He died of his injuries aged 38, the first Methodist martyr. He had been a generous supporter of Whitefield and John Wesley, and his death placed Whitefield in severe financial difficulties.

Above: Cefn-brith, commonly regarded as the birthplace of John Penry

On hearing of Seward's demise, Wesley wrote, 'Surely God will maintain his cause. Righteous art thou, O Lord!' Seward's grave, beneath a yew tree outside St Mary's Church, Cusop (HR3 5RF), just over the Herefordshire border from Hay, includes the words 'For me to live is Christ and to die is gain' (Philippians 1:21); the same text is on a memorial plaque inside the church.

David Griffiths (1792–1863) from Carmarthenshire sailed as a missionary to Madagascar in 1820. Driven out by persecution, he returned to Wales in 1842 and became minister of Ebenezer Congregationalist Chapel (HR3 5AX) in Newport Street (now 'The Globe at Hay'). He saw much fruit here, but Madagascar was never far from his heart. While at Hay he began to revise the Malagasy translation of the New Testament, and travelled extensively to speak of the island's needs. Griffith John, the missionary to China, married his daughter.

Llanafan Fawr

St Afan's Church (LD2 3PN) at Llanafan, between Newbridge-on-Wye and Beulah, contains a Welsh plaque near the burial place of Thomas Huet (died 1591), who helped Richard Davies and William Salesbury with the 1567 Welsh New Testament by translating Revelation.

Llangamarch Wells

A bilingual plaque on the wall below St Cadmarch's Church (LD4 4EE), almost opposite Llangamarch station, commemorates John Penry (1563–93). Penry is traditionally linked with Cefn-brith (LD4 4ES), a nearby farm – although he may have been from Glamorgan, related to the Penry family of Llanedi in Carmarthenshire.

A graduate of both Cambridge – a celebrated 'nursery' of Puritans – and Oxford, John Penry submitted a number of anguished treatises urging the authorities to take action to meet the spiritual needs of Wales. He was associated with the secret

John Penry's legacy

Although Penry spent little of his adult life in Wales, his writings reveal his deep concern for his native land. He lamented the lack of preachers and considered many of those who did preach to be 'blind guides'. Calling for more thorough reform of the church in order to facilitate evangelism, he particularly emphasized that the common people should hear the gospel in the Welsh language.

A week before his death in 1593 he wrote, 'I am a poor young man born and bred in the mountains of Wales . . . I leave the success of these my labours unto such of my countrymen, as the Lord is to raise up after me for the accomplishing of that work, which in the calling of my country

unto the knowledge of Christ's blessed Gospel I began.'

In the short term these words seemed to express a vain hope. Penry's actual contribution to the cause of the gospel in Wales was negligible. However, within 50 years Vavasor Powell, one of the leaders of the Welsh Puritan movement, could list Penry among his spiritual forefathers. With the evangelical revival beginning in the 18th century, Penry's heartfelt longing for the spread of the gospel here was remarkably fulfilled. Later generations of Nonconformists – especially Independents – came to regard him as the forerunner of Welsh Dissent and acclaim him as a hero and martyr.

press behind the satirical 'Martin Marprelate' tracts aimed at the ecclesiastical establishment and has been accused of being their author, although this is unlikely.

Having fled to Scotland for safety, he there turned from Presbyterianism to become a convinced Separatist in his view of the church. In 1592 he attached himself to Henry Barrow's Separatist congregation in London, intending ultimately '. . . to employ my small talent in my poor country of Wales, where I know that the poor people perish for want of knowledge.' However, at the age of 30 he was arrested and found guilty of treason at a disgracefully unjust trial. He left a widow and four young daughters.

Take the road from Llangamarch for Cefn Gorwydd and Tirabad. After half a mile (0.8 km), a low sign on the verge points left to Cefn-brith and Cynala. Climb the hill, and 0.6 miles (1 km) beyond Penrhiw farm, turn into the opening on the left (no sign). Go through the gate; there is a simple plaque on the porch by the front door.

Llansanffraid

The metaphysical poet Henry Vaughan (1621–1695) was born at Newton-by-Usk (LD3 7YG), now a private farm, on the left about a mile before Llansanffraid on the A40 from Brecon to Abergavenny. A Welsh-speaker, he studied at Oxford and London but returned to his native area to practise as a doctor. He was related to George Herbert, and described himself as

Above: *Trefeca-fach, home of Howel Harris and the 'Family'*
Below: *Howel Harris*

one of Herbert's 'pious converts'. Herbert's influence on his poetry is clear, though Vaughan's work has a more mystical strain:
I saw Eternity the other night,
Like a great ring of pure
and endless light,
All calm, as it was
bright . . .
My soul, there is a
country
Far beyond the stars
His Latin gravestone lies in the beautiful setting of the cemetery of St. Bridget's Church, Llansanffraid (LD3 7YF).

Talgarth and Trefeca

Talgarth and Trefeca have a special place in the history of Welsh Calvinistic Methodism. Trefeca-fach (LD3 0PP) was the home of Howel Harris (1714–73), one of its main founders. He was converted in 1735 at more or less the same time as Daniel Rowland and George Whitefield, although quite independently of them. Shortly afterwards he had a profound spiritual experience at Llangasty Tal-y-llyn Church (LD3 7PX), by the shores of picturesque Llangorse Lake/ *Llyn Syfaddan*, as a result of which he devoted himself to tireless itinerant evangelism. Although he suffered much at the hands of mobs organized by gentry and clergy, nothing could daunt his zeal for Christ and the gospel.

Doctrinal and personal tensions eventually arose between Harris and the other Methodist leaders, although they were later reconciled. In 1752 he established a self-supporting community – the 'Family' – at Trefeca-fach. His boundless evangelistic energy and personal dynamism, which included a potent blend of tenderness and authoritarianism, made him one of the most important Welshmen of his time.

Above: College Farm, Trefeca Isaf, the site of the Countess of Huntingdon's college for training preachers

The 'Family' continued at Trefeca after Harris' death, but in the 1830s the buildings were presented to the Calvinistic Methodists, and in 1842 a theological college was opened. It was transferred to Aberystwyth in 1906, but 'Coleg Trefeca' continued as a preparatory college and is now a lay training and conference centre (open to the public). Numerous items associated with Methodism and the 'Family' are on display, while the building dating from Harris' time is particularly fascinating.

For Coleg Trefeca, turn left on entering Trefeca on the B4560 from Talgarth. To reach Llangasty Tal-y-llyn, continue along the B4560; 1.6 miles (2.6 km) beyond Llan-gors, near Cathedine Church, take a sudden right turn down a lane (current sign: Beacons Nurseries), *then right and right again.*

Now known as College Farm (LD3 0PP), Trefeca Isaf between Trefeca and Talgarth is the site of Trefeca College, the Countess of Huntingdon's 'nursery for preachers' (quite distinct from the later college at Trefeca-fach). The first president was the godly John Fletcher of Madeley. There is a tradition that Williams Pantycelyn's hymn: 'Guide me, O Thou great Jehovah', was translated from the original Welsh for the opening in 1768, when Whitefield preached in front of the college building. On its first anniversary, John Wesley was the preacher.

After the countess's death in 1791, the college was transferred to Cheshunt and later amalgamated with Westminster College, Cambridge. Now a

Welsh Calvinistic Methodism

Howel Harris, Daniel Rowland, and William Williams were the three main pioneers of Calvinistic Methodism in Wales. Later leaders included Thomas Charles and John Elias, while Martyn Lloyd-Jones delighted in his Calvinistic Methodist heritage. 'Methodism' originally referred to a disciplined lifestyle, but was soon additionally linked with a vibrant experience of God's grace. Welsh Methodists were mainly Calvinistic in doctrine, holding that, while the gospel should be preached earnestly because all have a responsibility to repent and believe in Christ, salvation is the sovereign work of God. These three elements of Methodism were vividly expressed in the hymns of Williams Pantycelyn and Ann Griffiths; they were also evident in other contemporary figures – including George Whitefield and the Countess of Huntingdon in England, and Jonathan Edwards in America – who saw themselves as heirs of the Reformers and Puritans.

Wesleyan Methodism shared much with its Calvinistic counterpart, but placed more emphasis on the role of the human will in choosing to believe in Christ than on the sovereign work of God. It had little early impact on Wales, however, largely because John Wesley was unable to preach in Welsh.

Although both forms of Methodism originated within the Church of England, they eventually established separate denominations. The Welsh Calvinistic Methodists, formed in 1811, became the largest Nonconformist body here, but the awakening also had a powerful impact on the Independents and Baptists, and affected the life of Wales on a scale not seen since the 'Age of the Saints' in the 6th century.

private house, College Farm is not open to the public, but much of the original architecture can be seen from the roadside, including the neo-Gothic windows favoured by the countess.

College Farm is on the left, a few hundred yards along the road from Trefeca to Talgarth. There is a small space to pull off the road.

Howel Harris was converted at Talgarth Church (LD3 0BE). On Palm Sunday 1735 the vicar urged his parishioners to attend the Easter communion: 'You say that you are not fit to come to the Table. Well, then, I say that you are not fit . . . to live and neither are you fit to die.' These words caused Harris much agony of soul until Whit Sunday, when 'strength was given me to believe that I was receiving pardon on account of (Christ's) blood. I lost my burden: I went home leaping for joy.' Immediately he became an evangelist: 'I said to a neighbour who was sad, "Why are you sad? I know my sins have been forgiven."'

As he was not an ordained clergyman, Harris was not allowed to preach in churches and therefore took to the open air. One day in 1738 a young man heard him preaching in Talgarth churchyard and later recorded his experience, translated as follows:

This the morning I'll remember,
I myself heard heaven's call,
I received a fearful summons
From the highest court of all.

The young man was William Williams Pantycelyn; his life was changed that day, with untold consequences for himself and all those uplifted by the biblical truths and spiritual warmth of his hymns.

The church is at the top of The Bank by the town hall in the centre of Talgarth. From the porch take the narrow path diagonally across the churchyard for some 34 paces to Harris' father's low 'platform'

grave (on the left), where Harris would stand to preach; the inscription is now difficult to decipher.

RADNORSHIRE/SIR FAESYFED

Knucklas/Cnwclas

A simple modern plaque outside Knucklas Baptist Church (LD7 1PP) commemorates Vavasor Powell (1617–70), the indefatigable Welsh Puritan. According to an opponent, he was born in a tavern here, but his supporters claimed that his long-established family home was 'the best and ancientest house in the Burrow'. Converted through Puritan books and Walter Cradoc's ministry, he was soon in

Above: *Knucklas Baptist Church, with a memorial plaque to Vavasor Powell above the front door*

trouble for his uncompromising preaching. Under the 1650 Act for the Better Propagation and Preaching of the Gospel in Wales, he devoted himself to fearless itinerant evangelism and planting and nurturing Independent congregations – comprising Baptists and Paedobaptists – in mid-Wales. After the monarchy was restored in 1660, he spent much time in prison on account of his preaching. He died a prisoner in London and was buried in Bunhill Fields.

In his early years his zeal sometimes led him into intemperate words and actions, and his belief in the imminent return of Christ caused him much trouble. Towards the end of his life, however, he became more mature and measured, saying that 'I never trusted Christ without finding him faithful, nor my own heart without finding it false'. Through thick and thin his heartfelt concern for the spiritual welfare of Wales was never extinguished.

Knucklas is on the B4355 from Knighton to Newtown. Follow the sign for 'Village centre'. The tavern was located on the left, opposite some council houses. For the house standing on the more likely site of his birthplace, bear right by the Castle Inn, right again to cross a bridge, and walk up the steep lane (Castle Hill). 'Vavasour House' (LD7 1PR) – 'Vavasour' is an alternative but incorrect spelling for Vavasor – is the first house on the left. In private ownership, it offers excellent views of the spectacular 13-arch railway viaduct. Return to the Castle Inn, and turn right; the Baptist chapel is a short distance on the right.

Above: *Cae-bach Chapel (United Reformed Church), Llandrindod. The original building was associated with the ministry of Ioan Thomas*

Llandrindod Wells

Llandrindod grew as a spa town in Victorian times, but Christian witness in the area is much older. Just to the left of the main approach road to the lake is a reconstruction of the ground-plan of a medieval church, discovered nearby in the 1980s. It was probably built in the 12th century, but there is evidence of earlier religious activity. It is dedicated to Maelog, a 6th century Celtic saint engaged in evangelism in Powys and elsewhere. Information boards provide archaeological details and a tentative outline of Maelog's life.

More recently Cae-bach Chapel (LD1 6BY), attractive in its simplicity, was erected for an Independent congregation, probably in 1715 (rebuilt 1804). By the chapel there is a low building bearing the words

'Cae-bach Chapel Stable', where worshippers from the hill farms would tether their horses.

Ioan (John) Thomas (1730–1804?) ministered in the original building from 1767 to 1779; he also had charge of churches at Rhayader and Garn near Newbridge-on-Wye. A native of Myddfai, he was awakened through Howel Harris' preaching, and often invited Harris to preach at Cae-bach.

Among the first converts was Thomas Jones of Trefonen, later of Pencerrig (LD2 3TF) near Builth; his son, also named Thomas (1742–1803) became one of Wales' most renowned landscape painters. Both father and son were buried at Cae-bach.

Ioan Thomas knew times of revival here, although tensions arose because of his itinerant evangelism at the expense of his own congregation. In addition to some memorable Welsh hymns, he wrote *Rhad Ras* (Free Grace), the first autobiography in Welsh, published posthumously in 1810, it is notable for its rough-hewn style and vivid portrayal of contemporary Welsh Christianity.

At the far end of Llandrindod on the A483 to Newtown, turn left (sign: Industrial Estate/Police/Bus Station) and cross the railway. Just beyond a roundabout, a lane on the right leads to Cae-bach Chapel. Pencerrig is on the right, 4.5 miles (7.2 km) from Llandrindod on the A483 to Builth.

Since 1903 Llandrindod has been the home of the annual Keswick in Wales Convention, a source of encouragement to many. It originally met at the Albert Hall in Ithon Road, but subsequently moved to a pavilion facing Station Crescent and then to various chapels in the town. The venue is now the Pavilion Conference Centre near Holy Trinity Church (LD1 5EQ) in Spa Road.

Maesyronnen

In addition to its glorious views towards the Black Mountains, Maesyronnen Chapel (HR3 5NJ) has particular historical significance. The congregation was possibly established by Vavasor Powell as early as the 1640s and later benefited from the ministries of Henry Maurice (1634–82), the 'Apostle of Breconshire', and Rhys Prydderch (1620?–99). Originally a branch of the Llanigon church near Hay, which included both Independents and Baptists, it eventually became a congregation of Independents.

Registered in 1696 or 1697 following the 1689 Toleration Act, the chapel is one of the earliest Nonconformist buildings in Wales, and the oldest still used for worship. It was originally a 16th century 'tŷ hir' (long house), a farmhouse with an attached cow-shed; the latter became the chapel, with the house providing accommodation for the minister. Despite minor alterations over the years, the simplicity of the chapel exterior and interior clearly expresses the early Nonconformist approach to worship.

0.5 miles (0.8 km) from Glasbury on the A438 to Hereford, turn

Above: *Maesyronnen Chapel (United Reformed Church)*

left at the sign for Maesyronnen Chapel. Climb a steep hill for 0.5 miles (0.8 km); at another sign turn right down a short narrow lane. The chapel is normally closed during the week, but there are directions for obtaining a key.

Rhayader/Rhaeadr Gwy

'Rhaeadr Gwy' means 'The waterfall on the Wye'. This was removed when the bridge was built over the river in 1780, although there are impressive waterfalls at the reservoirs created by drowning the nearby Elan valley to provide water for Birmingham.

Near the bridge stands Tabernacle (LD6 5AG), a Congregational chapel erected in 1721 (rebuilt 1836). In 1767 Ioan Thomas came here as minister. Although more commonly associated with Llandrindod, in Welsh he is known as 'Ioan Thomas Rhaeadr Gwy'.

Robert Thomas became minister in 1839, and soon experienced a time of revival — around 100 were added to the church in 1841. His son, Robert Jermain Thomas, the martyr-missionary to Korea, was born here in 1840, although the family moved to Hanover Chapel, Llanofer, Monmouthshire, by the end of the decade.

From the clock in the centre of Rhayader, go down West Street into Bridge Street.

⑤ The South-East Corner
Protestants, Puritans, Preachers

The area from Cardiff and Caerphilly eastwards to the Severn bridges may not be the most strikingly beautiful in Wales. Nevertheless, there is no denying its historical and contemporary importance – or its spiritual significance – in the life of the nation

CARDIFF AND CAERPHILLY

Cardiff/Caerdydd

Cardiff is the largest city in Wales and its capital; it is also the seat of the National Assembly for Wales. Although the city has a long history, it was not until the arrival of industry in the 19th century, and especially the world-wide demand for coal from the south Wales valleys, that it began to experience significant growth.

It was here that Martyn Lloyd-Jones was born and that Evan Roberts spent his last years. However, Cardiff also has many other significant links with Christianity. Cathays Park (CF10 3ND) has been acclaimed as one of the finest civic centres in Europe. At its heart stands the magnificent Edwardian City Hall. A visit to its Marble Hall on the first floor provides an immediate picture of the history of Wales, for the eleven statues here represent heroes of Wales, chosen by public vote in 1916. They include four rulers (two kings, a prince and a queen), a rebel, a soldier, a bard, and four Christian leaders – a Celtic saint, a scholar, a Bible translator, and a preacher and hymn-writer. These are:

St David, 6th century, the patron saint of Wales.

Giraldus Cambrensis, 1146–1223, scholar and ecclesiastic in Norman times.

Bishop William Morgan, c 1545–1604, first translator of the Bible into Welsh (1588).

William Williams, 1717–91, Wales' finest hymn-writer.

Outside, and at the opposite corner of the park, stands a statue of John Cory (1828–1910). He and his brother Richard (1830–1914) were wealthy Cardiff industrialists. They owned collieries in the Rhondda, Ogmore Vale, Neath, and Aberdare; they were the largest wagon-owners in the UK, and their ships carried Welsh coal all over the world. They were also Christians:

Facing page: *Tintern Abbey, between Monmouth and Chepstow, in the beautiful Wye valley*

Above: Statue of John Cory,
Cathays Park

Richard was a Baptist and John
a Wesleyan Methodist. Their
philanthropy amounted to what
today would be the equivalent
of many millions of pounds.
All kinds of evangelical causes
benefited from their Christian
benevolence, including temperance
missions, Band of Hope Unions,
Dr Barnardo's, the YMCA, the
Soldiers' and Sailors' Rest and,
especially, the Salvation Army.

The Church of St John the
Baptist (CF10 1BH) near the
covered market is one of the
city's oldest remaining medieval
buildings, and is associated
with the very beginnings of
Nonconformity in Wales. In 1633
the vicar was William Erbery
(1604–54), a native of nearby
Roath. Both he and his curate

Walter Cradoc (1610?–59) were
associates of William Wroth
(1576–1641), the Puritan vicar of
Llanvaches in Monmouthshire.
The Bishop of Llandaff accused
Erbery and Wroth of being
'two noted schismatics' and in
1635 they were cited before the
Court of High Commission for
neglecting to read the Book of
Sports, not wearing a surplice,
and outdoor preaching. Erbery
eventually resigned his living,
Wroth conformed for the time
being, and Cradoc moved to
Wrexham. The three men were to
be associated again in the forming
of the first Independent church in
Wales at Llanvaches.

The pedestrian precinct from
the porch of St John's leads to
a junction with High Street. At
this point, in the middle of the
road, stood the old Town Hall
until it was pulled down in the
middle of the 18th century. Here,
on 7 March 1739, occurred a
significant meeting in the history
of the Methodist Revival in Wales.
George Whitefield, on his first
visit to Wales, had preached from
'the Judge's seat' in the hall, and
after the sermon Howel Harris
approached him. Both men were in
their mid 20s; they had previously
corresponded and each held the
other in the greatest respect.

Whitefield: 'When I first saw
him, my heart was knit closely to
him. I wanted to catch some of his
fire and gave him the right hand of
fellowship with my whole heart.'

Harris: 'The first thing he said
to me was, "Do you *know* your
sins are forgiven?" '

In St Mary's Street is the
House of Fraser department store,

Above: St David, by Sir William Goscombe John, City Hall

formerly James Howell's. Over 450 years ago it was the site of the cruel death of Rawlins White (c 1485–1555), a Cardiff fisherman and one of the three Welsh martyrs during the reign of the Catholic Queen Mary. He was illiterate but, having learned passages of the Bible read out to him, had become a Protestant. Arrested on suspicion of heresy and held in prison for a year, he refused to recant and was burned at the stake.

Bethany Chapel, the first home of the oldest English Baptist cause in Cardiff, was built in 1806 on the site where he was martyred. The chapel's structure was incorporated within the House of Fraser store in the 1960s.

Enter the store near the junction of St Mary's Street and Wharton Street. A commemorative plaque is to be seen on the wall at the back of the menswear department.

At the other end of Wharton Street is the Hayes, and a short distance from the junction stands

Tabernacl (Tabernacle) Welsh Baptist Church (CF10 1AJ). In September 1828, after two years at Caerphilly, Christmas Evans (1766–1838) accepted a call to be the third pastor of the church. He lived at 44 Caroline Street, just around the corner (currently part of the Red Onion fish and chip shop).

His time here was rather unhappy. His health was deteriorating and he was starting to feel his age; the disgraced previous minister (a drunkard and adulterer) persisted in attending the services and denying all guilt; and there were constant quarrels among church leaders. Eventually he returned to minister in north Wales. Nevertheless, during the four years he was here, 80 members were added to the church. The present building dates from 1868. Evans is commemorated by a plaque on an internal wall.

Caerphilly/Caerffili

Renowned for its castle and cheese, Caerphilly also has an important place in the early history of the Methodist Revival in Wales. In 1738 David Williams (1709–84), minister of the Independent church at Watford Chapel here, invited Howel Harris to preach to the scattered Dissenting groups of the Caerphilly area. (The building is now the home of Watford Congregational Church and Caerphilly Evangelical Church.) A local ironmaster, Thomas Price J.P. (1712–83) of Plas Watford, was converted at this time. There was always a welcome for Methodist preachers at Plas Watford, and the Wesley brothers often stayed here. In 1742 the 'New House' or 'New Room' was built at nearby Groes-wen for the local Methodist society. The early Methodists avoided such names as 'chapel' or 'meeting house' in order to avoid being thought of as Nonconformists. Groes-wen was the first building erected for worship by the Calvinistic Methodists in Wales; by 1851 the census of religious worship listed 330 of their chapels in south Wales alone.

On 5-6 January 1743 the first 'Association' met to define, regulate, and organize the Calvinistic branch of Methodism in England and Wales. Day-time meetings took place at the New Room, Groes-wen, while evening deliberations were held at Plas Watford, where all were accommodated. Six clergymen were present (including George Whitefield, Daniel Rowland, Howel Davies and William Williams) and twelve laymen (including Howel Harris and John Cennick). Four were Englishmen and the others Welsh. Whitefield was appointed moderator. It was decided that the laymen who preached were to call themselves not ministers but exhorters. By this time between 100 and 150 societies had been established in Wales, and responsibility for these, according to geographical location, was allocated to various exhorters. Howel Harris was to be the 'superintendent' of all the societies. He indeed had set up most of them, apart from those in and around Cardiganshire under Rowland's care.

The death of Rawlins White

'When he came to the place, where his poor wife and children stood weeping, the sudden sight of them so pierced his heart that the tears trickled down his face. Being come to the altar of his sacrifice, in going towards the stake, he fell down upon his knees, and kissed the ground; and in rising again, a little earth sticking on his face, he said these words, "Earth unto earth, and dust unto dust; thou art my mother, and unto thee I shall return" . . . Then some that stood by cried out, "Put fire! Set on fire!" which being done, the straw and reeds cast up a great and sudden flame. In which flame this good man bathed his hands so long, until such time as the sinews shrank, and the fat dropped away, saving that once he did, as it were, wipe his face with one of them. All this while, which was somewhat long, he cried with a loud voice, "O Lord, receive my spirit!" until he could not open his mouth. At last the extremity of the fire was so vehement against his legs, that they were consumed almost before the rest of his body was hurt, which made the whole body fall over the chain into the fire sooner than it would have done. Thus died this good old man for his testimony of God's truth, and is now rewarded, no doubt, with the crown of eternal life.' (From *Foxe's Book of Martyrs*)

Above: *Commemorative plaque in the House of Fraser store*

Take the A469 north from Cardiff towards Caerphilly. As the road bends downhill around Caerphilly Mountain, Watford Chapel stands on the right, just before a right turning to Watford. Set back a little, Plas Watford is the second house on the right along the road to Watford (CF83 1NE).

Whitefield had visited Plas Watford some two years before this Association meeting. On 14 November 1741 he had arrived there as a member of a wedding party, having that afternoon married Elizabeth James, a widow from Abergavenny; the wedding breakfast was provided by Thomas Price. The party had set out from Abergavenny two days before but had failed to find a clergyman sufficiently sympathetic to the despised Methodists to marry them. The Rev. John Smith of Capel Martin in Caerphilly was a friend of the Revival, and he had obliged. The present St Martin's Church (CF83 1EJ) was built in 1879 on the site of the old church.

Harris' preaching considerably

enlarged the congregation at Watford Chapel, but the Calvinism of the new converts was not acceptable to David Williams, and many of his members left to join the society at Groes-wen. Williams' grave lies within the chapel.

Go down the hill from Plas Watford and take the third turning right along St Martin's Road; the church is on the right.

At the junction of Tonyfelin Road and Bedwas Road in Caerphilly stand the two Tonyfelin Baptist Chapels (CF83 1PA). The present chapel was built in 1866; the original meeting house, now a private dwelling, is to its left. In August 1826, at 60 years of age, Christmas Evans arrived here from Anglesey to pastor the cause. His ministry at Caerphilly, although of only two years' duration, was his happiest period in south Wales. By the time he left, he had baptized and received 140 new converts into the church.

Turn left at St Martin's Church, down past the 13th century Caerphilly Castle (CF83 1JD). This is the largest castle in Britain after Windsor Castle; it is well worth a visit, even though it is a Norman castle built with the aim of subduing the Welsh! Continue to the centre of town and Tonyfelin Road.

Groes-wen

The present Groes-wen Chapel (CF15 7UR), on the outskirts of Caerphilly, was built in 1874 but the adjoining vestry and its horse-mounting block date from the 1742 'New House'. As well as being the first chapel built by the Methodists, it was also the first cause to separate from them. Howel Harris was determined that the movement should remain within the Established Church but this meant that, unless one of the few Methodist clergy happened to be in the area, members of the societies had to attend the parish church to receive communion; all christenings, weddings, and funerals had to be at the church; no society was to ordain one of its number to minister to its members. Such restraints were too much for the flourishing cause at Groes-wen: in 1745 it formed itself into an Independent church with William Edwards and Thomas William its co-pastors, much to Harris' disgust.

William Edwards (1719–89) was also the builder of the first chapel. He was born on a nearby farm but worked also as

Above: *Groes-wen Independent Chapel*

A wife for Christmas Evans!

Alone in his new home, Christmas Evans longed for a wife. His first wife, Catherine, had died in 1823. A local woman of some means was suggested. 'It isn't money I want, but a wife,' he answered. He eventually wrote to Mary Jones, his old housekeeper from Anglesey, proposing marriage. His friend, Thomas Davies, a minister at Argoed, agreed to act as mediator. He travelled with two saddled horses to Anglesey, preaching at various places, telling everybody that he was collecting a wife for Christmas Evans. The journey back took another week. Christmas was 61 and Mary 35. They were happily married for the remaining ten years of Evans' life. Out of respect for her husband's memory, Spurgeon secured a small grant for her in her widowed years, from an English Baptist fund.

CHRISTMAS EVANS.

a stonemason, and established a reputation as a bridge-builder. His most famous construction is the Old Bridge over the River Taff at Pontypridd, which he completed in 1754 at his fourth attempt. It remained the longest single-span bridge in Britain for 40 years. He went on to build many other chapels and is also credited with designing the new settlement of Morris-town (Morriston) for the employees of the Swansea copper works. He ministered at Groes-wen until he died in 1789, being known as 'the builder for both worlds'.

Groes-wen's most famous preacher was Griffith Hughes (1775–1839) who ministered here for over 40 years. In his time it became the mother-church of many Independent causes 'in a district extending from Merthyr Tydfil to Cardiff and from Bedwas to Efail Isaf'. He is buried in Groes-wen cemetery, along with so many other well-known names in the history of Welsh Independency, that the chapel is known as 'the Westminster Abbey of Wales'. Among them is Evan Jones, or 'Ieuan Gwynedd' (1820–52), minister, journalist and social reformer. He is remembered particularly for his well-argued response to the Anglican authors of the 'Blue Books' report on education in Wales in 1847, who went far beyond their remit in launching unfounded attacks on the Nonconformist chapels and the morals of the people.

Christmas Evans and his second wife Mary were married at St Ilan's Church (CF83 4JG), set on an almost deserted hillside beyond Groes-wen. William Edwards' grave is just outside and to the left of the church porch. There is also a mass grave for many of the victims of the Senghennydd mining disaster of 1913, when 439 miners at the Universal Colliery were killed after a gas explosion ripped through the underground workings. It remains the worst mining disaster in the UK, possibly the worst in the world. Some of the bodies were so mutilated that they could not be identified and were buried together here at Eglwysilan.

The church is some 2 miles (3.2 km) north-west of Groes-wen, along what becomes a narrow mountain road, with impressive views in all directions.

MONMOUTHSHIRE/SIR FYNWY

Caer-went

Christianity came to Wales by AD 200, during the days of the Roman Empire. The first Welsh Christian martyrs were Julius and Aaron, killed for their faith at Caerleon in the 3rd century. At Caer-went, mid-way between Chepstow and Newport on the A48, a Christian chapel from the Roman period has been discovered. Among the items found is a pewter vessel with the Chi Rho symbol scratched on it, perhaps used at 'agape' meals. Dated AD 375, it is the oldest Welsh Christian object and is

Left: Watford Independent Chapel, Caerphilly

Above: Plas Watford

now at Newport Museum, John
Frost Square, Newport (NP20 1PA).

Cwmyoy/Cwm-iou
The fascinating St Martin's
Church, Cwmyoy (NP7 7NT) –
'the most crooked church in Great
Britain' – was built on broken
rock foundations which, over
hundreds of years, have moved
and twisted the building into its
current amazing form. The curate
here from 1719–1772 was Thomas
Jones, the only clergyman in the
region known to Howel Harris
in 1737 as having 'the force of life
in his ministry'. Harris would
often plan his preaching journeys
so that he might have the benefit
of hearing Jones' evangelical
ministry, and the home at
Cwmyoy was always open to him
and other Methodist exhorters
on their travels. When Whitefield

Above: William Edwards

Above: *St Ilan's Church*

came here in 1739, 'the church not being quite large enough to hold half the congregation, I preached from the cross in the churchyard. The Word came with power.'

Take the minor road from Hay-on-Wye towards Llanvihangel Crucorney/Llanfihangel Crucornau, via the Gospel Pass and Capel-y-ffin. About 5 miles (8 km) south of Llanthony/Llanddewi Nant Hodni, a turning to the left leads to Cwmyoy.

Llangwm
About 1¼ miles (2 km) south of

Llangwm village stands Trefela (or Trebela) Farm where Walter Cradoc (1610?–59), friend of Richard Baxter, John Owen and Oliver Cromwell, and probably the greatest of the Welsh Puritans, was born. Two other notable Welsh Puritans, Morgan Llwyd and Vavasor Powell, were converted under his ministry. After a turbulent life of constant clashes with the Laudian Anglican establishment at Cardiff, Wrexham, Llanvaches and London, and then as an itinerant preacher and 'approver' of preachers under Cromwell, he

Right: *The twisted interior of St Martin's Church, Cwmyoy*

Robert Jermain Thomas: martyr-missionary to Korea

Thomas' original aim was to serve as a missionary in China. He set out in 1863 under the auspices of the London Missionary Society, but within a few months of arriving there his wife and young child died. Instead of returning home, he determined to take the gospel to Korea. In 1866, as the ship on which he was sailing made its way towards Pyongyang, it was attacked by the Koreans; he endeavoured to offer Bibles to the attackers, but was captured and killed.

However, these Bibles, together with portions of Scripture and tracts that he had already thrown to people along the river banks, were to have a remarkable spiritual influence on the people, leading to numerous conversions and the formation of groups of Christians. Even the man who killed him became a Christian, and some of this man's descendants became ministers of the gospel. Robert Thomas is widely regarded by Korean Christians as the man who brought the gospel to their land. In 1931 they built the Robert Jermain Thomas Memorial Church in Pyongyang in his honour (since closed by the communist government of North Korea). In their desire to honour his memory, Christians from Korea often visit Hanover Chapel, and generous support has also come from Korea for the Wales Evangelical School of Theology at Bryntirion, Bridgend.

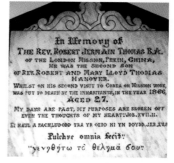

Robert Jermain Thomas plaque, Hanover Independent Chapel (now United Reformed Church), Llanover

returned to Llangwm as vicar of St Jerome's Church (NP15 1HA) in 1655. The lonely church, with its off-centre tower and 15th century rood screen, is in a beautiful location. Cradoc is buried under the floor of the chancel; no memorial remains to mark the grave.

St Jerome's Church stands in Upper Llangwm, about 3 miles (4.8 km) east of Usk on the B4235 towards Chepstow.

Llanover/Llanofer

At the far end of Llanofer village, just off the A4042 from Abergavenny towards Pontypool, stands Hanover Chapel (NP7 9HD). The present building was erected in 1839, although there was a chapel here from at least 1744, located in what is now the manse.

Its main interest, however, lies in its links with Robert Jermain Thomas (1840–66), the first Protestant missionary to take the gospel to Korea in modern times. He was born in Rhayader, but his father, Robert Thomas, became minister at Hanover Chapel in the late 1840s. Although altered to some extent, the current building is the one in which the family worshipped; their home at the nearby manse has recently been renovated. There are memorial plaques to him and his father inside the chapel.

Llanvaches/Llanfaches

William Wroth (1576–1641) was appointed rector of St Dubricius' Church at Llanvaches (NP26 3AY), between Newport and Chepstow, in either 1611 or 1617. About the year 1630 he was converted and for the next ten years so successful was his ministry that Llanvaches became known as 'the Jerusalem of Wales'.

Forced to resign his office as rector in 1638, in November 1639 Wroth formed a 'conventicle' at Llanvaches, the first Independent cause in Wales and the beginning of Welsh Nonconformity. Walter Cradoc had by now returned from Wrexham to assist Wroth, and William Erbery and Morgan Llwyd were also involved. It is thought that Cradoc was a member of Henry Jacob's Independent church at Southwark while he was in London. If so, this might explain why those at Llanvaches adopted the understanding of the nature of the church held by Jacob and others – also known as 'the New England way' because it was adopted by the Massachusetts Congregational churches – namely a congregation of 'visible saints' bound together by covenant to worship and serve Christ. It is interesting to note that Henry Jessey, the pastor of Jacob's church in 1639, came to assist in the formation of the new cause at Llanvaches. No church building was erected: the meetings

Above: St Jerome's Church, Llangwm. Walter Cradoc's grave is under the chancel floor

Above: St Dubricius' Church, Llanvaches. William Wroth's grave is below the porch floor

Below: Llanvaches Chapel commemorative stone. The original church was the first Nonconformist cause to be established in Wales

were held in surrounding houses and barns and, perhaps, still in the parish church itself.

When the Civil War broke out in 1642, the congregation was obliged to flee, first of all to Bristol and then to London. After the victory of the parliamentary army it was able to return and extend its influence to other parts of south-east Wales, partly through the evangelistic endeavours of the preachers whom it sent forth. The spiritual revival that accompanied this preaching was no doubt in Cradoc's mind when he reported in 1650 that 'I have observed and seen in the mountains of Wales the most glorious work that ever I saw… the gospel has run over the mountains between Breconshire and Monmouthshire as the fire in the thatch.'

William Wroth is buried under the porch of St Dubricius' Church. The Independent cause did not erect a chapel building until sometime before 1700, at nearby Carrow Hill (the other side of the A48). It moved to the present site, Tabernacle United Reformed Church (NP26 3BL), just off the A48, in 1802.

LLANVACHES CONGREGATIONAL CHAPEL 1639.

⑥ Glamorgan
Valleys of vision

To some, the industrialized 'Valleys' of Glamorgan and Monmouthshire are the essence of Wales. However, the old Glamorgan/Morgannwg, which included Cardiff and Caerphilly, also encompassed the very different 'Vale', Swansea and Gower. All these areas have witnessed the glory of the gospel

The Glamorgan Valleys

There were early Dissenters in the sparsely populated uplands of Glamorgan and Monmouthshire from *c* 1650, nurtured by Vavasor Powell (1617–70) and Henry Maurice (1634–82). In 1743 Henry Davies (1696?–1766), built the first Nonconformist chapel in the Rhondda at Cymer. The rapid development of the coal industry in the later 19th century led to an increasing number of chapels to meet the spiritual needs of the new inhabitants.

William Evans (1795–1891), 'the silver bell of Tonyrefail', preached at the opening of many of them. Salvation Army and other missions in the Rhondda, associated with Pamela Shepherd ('Mother Shepherd', 1836–1930) and Rosina Davies (b. 1866), produced great spiritual harvests. Under Alfred Ollivant (1798–1882), the evangelical bishop of Llandaff, the Church Extension Society ensured a significant increase of new churches and clergy. In Tredegar and then Pontypridd, John Pugh (1846–1907) exercised an awakening ministry that led to the Calvinistic Methodists' Forward Movement to promote evangelism among the working population. During the 1904 Revival, many Nonconformist preachers, such as R. B. Jones, Porth, O. M. Owen, Merthyr, and W. S. Jones, Llwynypia, exercised fruitful ministries.

Llangynwyd

Rich in history, this hilltop village has a number of interesting buildings in the vicinity of the churchyard, including the church itself and Bethesda Independent Chapel, built in the late 1790s and still testifying to the unadorned simplicity of Nonconformist worship.

Samuel Jones (1628–97) of Chirk, Denbighshire, was appointed as vicar here in 1657,

Facing page: Worm's Head, Gower Peninsula

From Junction 36 on the M4 take the dual carriageway northwards, signposted Maesteg. Turn right when it joins the A4063. After passing through Tondu and Coytrahen, turn right immediately after the entrance to the Georgia Pacific factory for Brynllywarch (a working farm). The A4063 continues northwards to Pont-rhyd-y-cyff, where a left turn leads to Llangynwyd ('Llan').

Above: John Evans, Eglwys-bach

Top: Brynllywarch Farm

Nantyffyllon (Maesteg)

Nantyffyllon is a former mining community on the A4063 north of Maesteg. During the 1904 Revival the Jeffreys brothers were converted at Shiloh Welsh Congregational Chapel here (CF34 0BS). In 1914 George Jeffreys (1889–1962) established the first Elim Pentecostal Church, the beginning of the Elim Foursquare Gospel Alliance which now has over 500 churches in Britain and 9,000 worldwide. He left the movement in 1939 because of his support for British Israelism. His elder brother, Stephen (1876–1943), exercised a similar Pentecostal ministry but travelled more extensively, visiting North America, Africa and the Antipodes. From 1926 he too left the Elim organization, preferring to work with the newly-formed Assemblies of God movement. He, like Samuel Jones, is buried at Llangynwyd – two very different bedfellows.

Pontypridd

Situated at the confluence of the rivers Taff and Rhondda, Pontypridd was one of the most important valley towns during

having been approved as a suitable candidate by Cromwell's 'Triers'. Deprived of his living by the Act of Uniformity of 1662, he established an 'academy' at Brynllywarch Farm nearby – the first Dissenting academy in Wales, indeed its first 'university' of sorts, at a time when Nonconformists were not allowed to study at the universities in England. Jones taught here for 35 years, preparing young men for the ministry as well as preaching to small congregations locally. He is buried in Llangynwyd churchyard (CF34 9SB), said to be the biggest private cemetery in Europe.

Above: The Old Bridge, Pontypridd, with Tabernacl Baptist Chapel and, behind it, the Eglwys-bach Memorial Chapel

the heyday of the coal industry. Its renowned bridge was built by William Edwards, the first minister of Groes-wen Independent Church. Behind the bridge stands Tabernacl Welsh Baptist Chapel (CF37 4PE), now a museum of local history and culture. An event here in April 1925 became national news when a 25 year-old doctor was invited to speak to a conference of the Union of Welsh Societies. This was the first public address in Wales by Martyn Lloyd-Jones, two years before he began his ministry at Aberavon. His analysis of the spiritual malady at the heart of 'The Problem of Modern Wales' was such that the pastor of Tabernacl, who was to second a vote of thanks, proceeded to disagree profoundly with him!

Pontypridd was the last field of service of John Evans (1840–97), the most famous Welsh Wesleyan minister and evangelist of his day. He ministered in 11 different circuits, and without doubt thousands were converted through his preaching. Known as John Evans, Eglwys-bach, from his birthplace in Denbighshire, he came to Pontypridd in 1893 to establish a Welsh-speaking Wesleyan Mission to the south Wales valleys. When he died, a public appeal raised sufficient money to build the Eglwys-bach Memorial Chapel (CF37 4SH) – now a surgery – in Berw Road, behind the museum.

Porth

The two Rhondda rivers meet at Porth, a few miles from Pontypridd. When Rhys Bevan Jones (1869-1933) came to Salem here in 1899, he joined a group of Rhondda Baptist ministers who met to pray for revival. Sometime before November 1904 – the date usually given for the beginning of the 1904 Revival – he and others in the valleys had known powerful effects of the Holy Spirit attending their preaching, and in early November revival came to Rhosllannerchrugog, near Wrexham, through his ministry there. It is quite misleading to use the often-heard phrase 'Evan Roberts's Revival' because the awakening was a work of God that had begun quietly, in various places, some months previously and was to break out more powerfully, and in many more locations, from the November onwards.

R B Jones subsequently ministered at Ainon Baptist Church, Ynys-hir, and at Tabernacle Baptist Church, Hannah Street, Porth (CF39 9PU), to a congregation of over a thousand. In addition to preaching at conventions and taking missions throughout Wales, he established a resident Bible Training School at Tynycymer Hall, Porth (CF39 9DE). At times up to 50 students would be pursuing studies here, and many went as missionaries throughout the world. Numerous well-known evangelicals – including Christabel Pankhurst, T T Shields, Martyn Lloyd-Jones, Robert Dick Wilson, and Gresham Machen – came here to address the students.

In 1936, after the death of R B Jones, the school was re-established by B S Fidler (1880–1970) as the Barry School of Evangelism, later called the South Wales Bible College. In 1985 it became the Evangelical Theological College of Wales, situated at Bryntirion, Bridgend, and since 2006 known as the Wales Evangelical School of Theology – WEST.

THE VALE OF GLAMORGAN/BRO MORGANNWG

Fonmon/Ffwl-y-mwn

Fonmon Castle (CF62 3ZN), dating from the early 13th century, is a fascinating building (open to the public; guided tours available). Philip Jones (1618–74), Oliver Cromwell's greatest supporter in Wales, lived here from 1656 onwards; the present owner is a direct descendant. Jones was a colonel in the parliamentary army during the Civil War, and as governor of Swansea successfully held the town against the royalist forces. He sat in the House of Commons 1650–1656, became comptroller of Cromwell's household, and superintended his funeral in 1658. Jones died at Fonmon and is buried in Penmark Church (CF62 3BP).

His great-grandson, Robert Jones (1706?–42), was converted through the ministry of Charles Wesley. The Wesley brothers often stayed at Fonmon, and Jones' influence as MP for Glamorgan enabled him to arrange many preaching opportunities for them in nearby churches.

From Cardiff, make for Cardiff Airport and bypass it by following the A4226/B4265 towards Llantwit

Major. Ignore the left turn to Fonmon (village); instead, continue for a short distance and turn left for Rhoose/East Aberthaw. Just afterwards, turn left into Castle Road and cross the junction at the traffic lights. The castle gates are on the left; the road continues to Penmark. Venture along lanes from Fonmon – or make for St Nicholas on the A48 between Cardiff and Cowbridge and follow the signs there – to Dyffryn House and Gardens (CF5 6SU).

Dyffryn House and Gardens have been called 'the grandest and most outstanding Edwardian gardens in Wales'. This was the home of John Cory of Cardiff from 1891 onwards; now owned by the National Trust, it is open to the public.

Above: *St Canna's Church, Llan-gan*

Llan-gan

Llan-gan is a pretty village, typical of many in the Vale of Glamorgan. In 1768, through the influence of the evangelical Countess of Huntingdon – Lady Selina, a prominent supporter of the evangelical revival – the living of Llan-gan Church (CF35 5DW) was obtained for David Jones (1736–1810). He became the leader of the Welsh Calvinistic Methodists after the deaths of the pioneers – the connecting link between the days of Daniel Rowland and those of Thomas Charles. Still more important, he was one of the sweetest and most melting of all Welsh preachers. Large crowds from the surrounding area would gather on the Communion Sunday morning to hear 'the Angel of Llan-gan'.

In 1775, he built Salem Chapel, Pen-coed (CF35 5LY), a few miles to the north, for the use of the Methodist societies that he had established; Sinah, his first wife, is buried in its cemetery. In 1780 he moved to Pembrokeshire; his grave lies in the churchyard at Manorowen, near Fishguard.

On the A48 from Cowbridge towards Bridgend, turn right at Pentre Meyrick and then left for Llan-gan.

Llantwit Major/Llanilltud Fawr

The correct name of this fascinating little town, full of buildings of historical interest, is Llanilltud Fawr. The English corruption, 'Llantwit Major', is a source of grief to those who speak Welsh. 'Llan' has come to mean 'church', and most place names beginning with 'llan' follow it with the name of the saint who planted the church. Here therefore is the church of Illtud (c475–c525), one of the key figures in early Welsh Christianity. Unfortunately, the best that the English settlers of the 12th century (and all centuries since) could do with 'Illtud' was 'twit'!

Illtud established his famous school here c 500. 'The earliest centre of learning in Britain', it became the centre of evangelical learning, faith, and prayer for the whole of Wales. Many of the Celtic saints – including Samson (c 485–565), Paul Aurelian (late 5th century), Gildas (c 500–c 570), and David (d 589?) – are said to have studied here. Its influence was not restricted to Wales: men were sent out to preach the gospel in other Celtic lands, namely Ireland, Cornwall, and Brittany.

The difference between the Catholic and the Celtic form of monasticism is worth remembering. The Catholics required their monks to be celibate and to reside in a monastery under the authority of an abbot, whereas Celtic monks could marry, live and preach in the community, and pass on their land within the family. Dating from the 9th to the 11th centuries, the Celtic stones and crosses now in the Galilee Chapel here testify to the widespread influence of the 'clas' (chapter) of Llanilltud up to the 12th century, when the Norman Church transferred the ownership of all tithes and land to Tewkesbury Abbey (Gloucestershire).

Although it dates from medieval times, the present church (CF61 2SB) may well be located on the site of Illtud's church and school. John Wesley preached here in 1777 and commented, 'One end of it is now in ruins. I suppose it has been abundantly the most beautiful, as well as the most spacious, church in Wales.'

St Athan/Sain Tathan

John Williams (1728–1806) was the first secretary and Thomas William (1761–1844) the first minister of Bethesda'r Fro ('Bethesda of the Vale') Chapel (CF62 4NG). Known as 'the Hymn-writers of Bethesda'r Fro', they were responsible for some memorable hymns still sung today. The founding of the church is bound up with the sad story of the Calvinistic Methodists' excommunication of Peter Williams, the Bible commentator, in 1791. Because of their sympathy for their old friend, the two men withdrew from the Methodists and formed

Above: Plaque on St Illtud's Church, Llantwit Major

an Independent cause here. Thomas William's grave is in the cemetery outside the simple little chapel; John Williams is buried at St Athan's Church (CF62 4PL).

From Llantwit Major take the B4265 towards Barry. Just after passing beneath a railway bridge turn left towards Eglwys Brewis. After less than a mile the small white chapel is to be seen on the right, bordering on the St Athan airfield.

Above: *Bethesda'r Fro Independent Chapel (now United Reformed Church)*

St Fagans/Sain Ffagan

Wales' National History Museum at St Fagans chronicles the historical lifestyle, culture, and architecture of the Welsh people. One of the largest open-air museums in Europe, it ranks among the UK's major free attractions. The influence of Christianity in Wales may be seen on every hand: the 13th century Llandeilo Tal-y-bont Church; Pen-rhiw Chapel, an old barn converted into a typical chapel (although in this case embracing Unitarianism); the exhibits on 'Religion in Wales' in the permanent indoor exhibition.

From M4 Junction 33 take the A4232 southwards. The entrance to Wales' National History Museum (CF5 6XB) is on the left after 2 miles (3 km).

WESTERN GLAMORGAN

Aberavon/Aberafan

Bethlehem Evangelical Church, Sandfields (SA12 6NE), was founded in 1914 by the Calvinistic Methodists' Forward Movement. The minister 1927–38 was Dr Martyn Lloyd-Jones (1899–1981), who lived with his young family at No. 57 and then at No. 28 Victoria Road. If ever in his long ministry he experienced revival, it was in these years at Aberavon, when over 500 people were converted 'from the world'.

Travelling westward on the M4, leave at Junction 40. Take the first exit from the roundabout, and turn right at the traffic lights into Talbot Road. At the next roundabout take the second exit (sign: Green Park Industrial Estate). Just before a large sign for the next roundabout, turn right into Afan Way for the chapel. Beyond the chapel, go through two sets of traffic lights into Victoria Road; No. 57 is on the right and No. 28 on the left.

Ilston/Llanilltud Gŵyr

The village's Welsh name – 'The Church of Illtud on Gower' – indicates that the church here is

Dr Martyn Lloyd-Jones (1899–1981)

The story of Martyn Lloyd-Jones is quite fascinating. Born in Cardiff, he grew up at Llangeitho in rural Ceredigion. After a brilliant career as a doctor, he gave up life in Harley Street to become a minister of the gospel. In his ministry he placed particular emphasis on the robust biblical Christianity that had exerted such a powerful influence on Wales in the past. Another prominent note was the need for true spiritual revival. Growing up at Llangeitho had given him an awareness of what God had done through Daniel Rowland in the 18th century. At Aberavon he experienced something of the same kind of revival, and he continued to emphasize the importance of an outpouring of the Holy Spirit for the rest of his life.

It is as a preacher, however, that he is chiefly remembered. 'Theology on fire' was his definition of preaching, and there is no better description of his own authoritative ministry. He is often regarded as the greatest preacher of the 20th century, and his books (based on his sermons) are in much demand throughout the world.

Although he moved to Westminster Chapel, London, in 1938, Wales was always close to his heart. He died on St David's Day 1981, longing to see his own nation returning to the faith of her fathers and experiencing the reality of God's presence in true revival.

See also in this series: Travel with Martyn Lloyd-Jones – the distinguished Welsh evangelist, pastor and theologian, by Philip Eveson.

Martyn Lloyd-Jones in his late 30s

associated with Illtud, one of the major figures of early Christianity in Wales through his theological school at Llantwit Major.

But Ilston – a corruption of Illtudston – has another claim to fame in the history of Welsh Christianity. During the Protectorate of Cromwell, the rector here was John Miles (1621–83). He held Baptist principles, and in gathering about him a congregation with similar beliefs, in 1649 he established the first Baptist church in Wales. By 1660, at the restoration of the monarchy, his church numbered about 250. Tradition has it that it used to meet also at the site of an old Pre-Reformation chapel lower down Cwm Ilston. The remains of this building may be seen a short distance along the path to the left of the Gower Inn car park, Parkmill (SA3 2EQ); a memorial plaque was placed here in 1928.

Through Miles' influence, other Baptist churches were founded in south Wales in the early 1650s. Because of persecution after 1660, Miles and many of his congregation fled to America and established a settlement in Massachusetts, calling it Swansey.

St Illtud's Church, Ilston (SA2 7LD) is a pleasant walk about a mile (1.6 km) further along the lane mentioned above; it may also be approached by car along the B4271 from Upper Killay.

Loughor/Casllwchwr
Moriah Chapel (SA4 6QZ), with its memorial to the 1904 Revival and Evan Roberts (1878–1951), stands in the centre of Loughor – strictly speaking in Carmarthenshire – on the A484 from Swansea. Here, on 31 October 1904, Roberts told the 15 young people present of his conviction that God would bless his church with a powerful visitation of the Holy Spirit. By the following Sunday night Moriah was full and revival had come to Loughor. At his home, 'Island House' (SA4 6TE), Roberts had already experienced seasons of profound communion with God during the months preceding the revival. His grave is in the family plot behind Moriah.

From Moriah, turn right at the war memorial, then second left into Bwlch Road. The road leads towards the River Loughor and eventually passes 'Island House' on the right.

Newton
Frances Ridley Havergal (1838–79), the poetess and hymn writer, spent the last eight months of her life at Park Villa, the home of her sister Maria, overlooking lovely Caswell Bay. Maria describes Frances at home: 'at her study

Left: Memorial to Ilston Baptist Church, the first Baptist cause in Wales

I could not do without Thee,
I cannot stand alone,
I have no strength or goodness,
No wisdom of my own;
But Thou, beloved Saviour,
Art all in all to me,
My power in every weakness,
My all-sufficiency.

There is a memorial plaque to her in Paraclete Church. See also in this series: *Travel with Frances Ridley Havergal – the English hymn writer and poet* by Carol Purves.

The B4593 climbs from Oystermouth towards Caswell Bay. Park Villa – a private dwelling, now called 'Havergal House' (SA3 4RU) – stands on the right, at the junction with Caswell Avenue. At the other end of Caswell Avenue, turn right into Summerland Lane; Paraclete Church is on the right, at the junction with Newton Road.

Above: *1904 Revival memorial at Moriah Presbyterian Chapel, Loughor*

table (where) she read her Bible by seven o'clock in summer and eight o'clock in winter; her Hebrew Bible, Greek Testament, and lexicons being at hand.' Though ill and weak, she led Bible classes for the local cottage-women and children at her home, in the village school, and at Paraclete Congregational Church (SA3 4ST) in Newton, where she and her sister worshipped. She also set up the 'Newton Temperance Regiment' for the boys of the village. The month before she died, Ira D. Sankey and his wife visited her. Many of her hymns are well-known – for example: 'Take my life and let it be / Consecrated, Lord, to Thee' and 'Who is on the Lord's side?' In the following verse she expresses a truth evidently displayed in her own short life:

Swansea/Abertawe
According to Dylan Thomas, Swansea is 'an ugly, lovely town . . . crawling, sprawling . . . by the side of a long and splendid curving shore.' Its rich Christian history meant little to him, and it is unlikely that he was aware of the significance of three churches (originally Baptist, Anglican, and Independent) standing within 100 yards of one another in the Dyfatty area, near Swansea railway station.

Bethesda Welsh Baptist Chapel (SA1 2EX), now an NSPCC centre, was built in 1831. Its most famous minister was Joseph Harris (1773–1825), known as 'Gomer'. The son of a

Above: *Havergal House, Newton*

drover, he was converted during a period of revival in Puncheston, Pembrokeshire, and in 1800 arrived to pastor the small Baptist cause at Swansea. Known as 'The Father of Welsh Journalism', in 1814 he began to publish what was to be the first Welsh weekly newspaper, *Seren Gomer* ('The Star of Gomer'). This paper, including its later metamorphosis to a quarterly Baptist magazine, became the longest-lived Welsh-language periodical, the last issue being published in 1983. He also helped to translate John Gill's New Testament Commentary into Welsh. For all his literary endeavours, however, Gomer emphasized that the work of preaching was 'the sweetest pleasure of his mind and the greatest happiness of his heart'.

His friend, Christmas Evans, was on a preaching tour when, on 19 July 1838, he died suddenly. Evans had preached twice the previous Sunday at Bethesda, and at Mount Pleasant Church, Swansea, on the Monday evening. He was taken ill that night and died from heart failure on the Thursday morning. His gravestone, with its thin, tall pillar, is in Bethesda cemetery and serves also as the gravestone for Harris himself.

In High Street stands the former St Matthew's Church (SA1 1LW) – until 1874 called St John's – now a Cyrenians Community Centre. Ambrose Mostyn (1610–63) was appointed vicar in 1646, and his preaching was such that Swansea 'later became the greatest stronghold of Welsh Nonconformity'. Greatly respected by other Puritan leaders, in 1648 he was sent as a preacher to north Wales.

A still more important Puritan was Stephen Hughes (1622–88), a native of Carmarthen who came to Swansea after being

Griffith John

Griffith John's life in China provides one of the most remarkable examples of 19th century missionary histories. With the Chinese people, he went through the Opium War, Taiping Rebellion, Japanese Wars and Boxer Rebellion, remaining at his post for over 50 years. After arriving in Shanghai he quickly learnt the language and was preaching in the streets within six months. In 1861 he moved to the inland city of Hankou (now Wuhan) in the province of Hubei. He was the first Protestant missionary to settle in Central China (doing so eight years before Hudson Taylor). In addition to preaching the gospel and planting churches, by 1899 Griffith John had built in Hankou: primary and secondary schools, two hospitals, a training college for teachers, and a Bible College. When he returned to Britain in 1911, gravely ill, he left behind in the provinces of Hubei and Hunan hundreds of Christian churches with a total membership of over 100,000. His first hospital has evolved into the present Union Hospital which serves the 10 million inhabitants of Wuhan. At its entrance stands a bust of Griffith John, placed by the Chinese to commemorate its founder. In 2012, the 100th anniversary of his death, the hospital commissioned and presented a replica of this bust to Swansea Museum (SA1 1SN), where it remains on permanent display.

ejected from Meidrim Church, Carmarthenshire, in 1662 because of his refusal to be bound by the requirements of the Act of Uniformity. As an ejected minister, he had no authority at St John's; however, his home was licensed for preaching and, as it also was in High Street, no doubt many of Mostyn's congregation were among his hearers. It is estimated that as many as 300–400 Dissenters lived in the town at that time. From Swansea he continued his preaching tours, visiting the many churches he had established in the west.

Swansea was also the ideal place for Hughes to resume his literary activities, in cooperation with Thomas Gouge and Charles Edwards. He published a number of editions of the influential verses of Rhys Prichard, vicar of Llandovery, including a comprehensive collection in 1681 to which he gave the title *Cannwyll y Cymry* ('The Candle

Above: *The grave of Christmas Evans outside the former Bethesda Baptist Chapel, Swansea*

of the Welsh'). He also published a cheap edition of the Welsh Bible (1677), and helped to produce a translation of *The Pilgrim's Progress* into Welsh (1688). He is buried in St Matthew's graveyard although the site is unknown.

Around the corner from St Matthew's, in Ebenezer Street, is Ebenezer Baptist Church (SA1 5BJ), formerly a Welsh Independent chapel. David Davies (1763–1816), from Llangeler, Carmarthenshire, erected the first building here in 1803. Known as the 'Silver Trumpet' because of his magnificent voice and the power of his preaching, he has a claim to being one of the greatest preachers among the Welsh Independents, and is a typical example of a Dissenting minister caught up in the fire of the Methodist Revival. During the 26 years of his ministry, having been pastor over four churches, he received over 2,000 people into church membership.

In one of the streets behind Ebenezer, Griffith John (1831–1912), one of the greatest of Welsh missionaries, was born in 1831. Converted at Ebenezer as a boy aged nine, he became known as 'The Boy-Preacher of Wales'. A bright future as a popular preacher lay before him, but he received a different calling: in 1855 he and his wife sailed under the auspices of the London Missionary Society to China. He is buried in Sketty cemetery (SA2 9BJ); his grave is on the line of the path passing the front of the church, some 15 yards beyond the church wall.

❼ Carmarthenshire
Fertile soil, faithful saints

While the eastern part of Carmarthenshire/Sir Gaerfyrddin has a fascinating industrial history, the rest of the county is noted for its attractive coastline, rolling countryside, and thriving agriculture. Christianity has borne much fruit here in this 'Garden of Wales'

SOUTHERN CARMARTHENSHIRE

Abergwili

In 1542 William Barlow transferred his bishop's palace from St David's to Abergwili, re-using the premises of an older priests' college. The building contains a chapel added in 1625 by William Laud – later the anti-puritan Archbishop Laud – when he was bishop.

Of all the bishops of St David's who resided at Abergwili, Wales has greatest cause to be grateful to Richard Davies (1501?–81). A convinced Protestant, he fled to Frankfurt during Mary's reign. After her death he returned and in 1561 was appointed bishop of St David's. In 1563 he invited William Salesbury (1520?–84?), a native of Llansannan but then living in Llanrwst, to Abergwili. Salesbury was a fine scholar, and in 1567 the outcome of his partnership with Davies and Thomas Huet was the first Welsh New Testament – which was

to provide the basis of William Morgan's translation of the whole Bible in 1588 – together with the first Welsh edition of the Book of Common Prayer. The building – open to the public – now houses the Carmarthenshire County Museum (SA31 2JG).

Abergwili lies on the A40 about a mile (1.6 km) east of Carmarthen.

Ammanford/Rhydaman
In 1904 the minister of Bethany Welsh Calvinistic Methodist Church, Wind Street, Ammanford (SA18 3DR), was W Nantlais Williams (1874–1959). 'Nantlais' was already a well-known name in Wales, largely through his winning eisteddfod chairs for his poetry. His burning ambition was to be a preacher-bard. However, on 6–7 November 1904 Joseph Jenkins (1861–1929) of Newquay, Cardiganshire, visited Bethany for two days of preaching services. The effect of his sermons, and of the prayer meetings held throughout the following week, was such that scores of men and

Facing page: The Upper Tywi Valley

women were converted. Not until the end of the week was the minister himself converted! This 'great week of the Revival for us in Ammanford' was the very next week after Evan Roberts' meetings at Moriah in Loughor.

Nantlais remained at Bethany for 44 years, and was one of the few Welsh Presbyterian ministers who laboured for the true gospel against the liberalism and modernism of his day. When he retired in 1944, his place was taken by J D Williams (1915–2006), who continued as minister until his own retirement in 1981. Under these two men Bethany received 77 years of faithful evangelical ministry.

Carmarthen/Caerfyrddin

Carmarthen town has a long history, much of which is of particular interest to the Christian.

The sad backdrop to the Carmarthen County War Memorial on Priory Street (SA31 1NA) is the old Priory Street Infirmary, derelict since 1996. On this site until 1857 stood the Queen Elizabeth Grammar School, founded in 1576, one of the oldest and best-known free grammar schools in Wales. A number of those mentioned in these pages received some of their education here, including Rhys Prichard, the 'Old Vicar' of Llandovery; Stephen Hughes; Griffith Jones (1683–1761), vicar of Llanddowror; and Peter Williams. One former pupil who will receive no further mention here is Beau Nash (1674–1761), the dandy of Bath and Tunbridge Wells.

Still standing is the site of the old Presbyterian College – now Carmarthen Evangelical Church – on the Parade (SA31 1LY) See picture on page 96. It can trace its origins to the dissenting academy opened c 1704 by William Evans (d 1718), minister of an Independent cause in the town. No other college or academy in Wales can compare with it for its wanderings, both geographical and theological. Its main financial support came from the Presbyterian Fund Board in London, and when a tutor died the academy would be transferred to the home of his appointed successor. Thus, from 1704 to 1795 it meandered from Carmarthen to Llwyn-llwyd (near Hay), to Haverfordwest, back to Carmarthen, then to Swansea, until settling finally back again in Carmarthen in 1795.

It moved to this site on the Parade in 1859 and remained open until 1963. Thoroughly Calvinistic, William Evans translated the *Westminster Confession of Faith* into Welsh, but subsequent tutors included Calvinists, Arminians, Arians, and Unitarians. Students destined for Baptist, Independent, Presbyterian, Unitarian, Calvinistic Methodist, and even Anglican ministries were prepared here. They included Thomas Charles (1755–1814) of Bala, Caleb Morris (1800–65) of Fetter Lane, London, and Michael Jones (1787–1853), first principal of Bala Independent Theological College.

At the end of the Parade is Parade Road, which leads to St Peter's Church (SA31 1LH). On

Above: *The Bishop's Palace, Abergwili (now Carmarthenshire County Museum)*

the south wall stands a tablet commemorating Dr Robert Ferrar, bishop of St David's, who on 30 March 1555 was burnt at the stake in the town's old market-place (Nott Square), along King Street from St Peter's. He had preached in this church often and part of his trial for heresy took place here. Strangely enough, Ferrar had angered his canons in St David's for not being sufficiently zealous in promoting reformation as they understood it, and by the time Mary Tudor came to the throne they had found a way to commit him to prison.

To Mary, however, he was the leader of the Protestant troublemakers in Pembrokeshire; on his refusal to recant, she sent him to the stake as an example to others. A small memorial placed within the rails of a monument to the soldier Sir William Nott marks the site of his death (SA31 1PQ). See also in this series: *Travel with the Martyrs of Mary Tudor*, by Andrew Atherstone.

From Nott Square the main road leads past the Guildhall into Lammas Street. On the left is Lammas Street Independent Chapel (SA31 3AP), the oldest Dissenting cause in Carmarthen, established *c* 1660. The first building on this site was erected in 1726.

The Nonconformists of the county owe their origins to the endeavours of Stephen Hughes (1622–88), 'the Apostle of Carmarthenshire'. Born in Carmarthen, he served as vicar of Meidrim 1655–1662; unwilling to accept the requirements of the Act of Uniformity, he was then ejected from his living and moved to Swansea. He travelled extensively throughout Carmarthenshire, preaching to the scattered Nonconformist congregations. Around 1658 he began the great work of his life, namely publishing Puritan books in Welsh. His Nonconformist beliefs notwithstanding, he was responsible for the publication of the verses of Rhys Prichard,

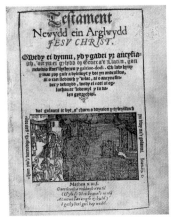

Above: *Title page of the first Welsh New Testament, 1567*

vicar of Llandovery, because he recognized their value in instructing the common people in basic biblical truths.

Opposite Lammas Street Chapel and to the right is the entrance to Water Street, the location of Water Street Welsh Presbyterian Chapel (SA31 1PZ). The first chapel on this site was built by Peter Williams (1723–96), the youngest of the founding fathers of Welsh Calvinistic Methodism, in his own garden. By 1743 he had been a student for three years at the grammar school and had proved himself a fine scholar and classicist. In that year he was converted while hearing George Whitefield preaching in the open air in Lammas Street. He served as a curate in various places in south Wales but, because of his Methodism, was never ordained.

His greatest contribution was 'Peter Williams' Bible' – successive editions of the 1588 Welsh Bible with what was generally a very helpful commentary on each chapter. Printed by John Ross in Carmarthen, this was the first Bible to be produced within Wales. Many thousands of copies were distributed from 1770 onwards. He also published the first Welsh concordance to appear in Wales. In 1790 a storm broke out over allegations that his comments on John 1:1 taught Sabellianism – a confusing of the distinctions between the persons within the Godhead – and he was excommunicated by the Methodists in 1791. His grave lies in the cemetery of Llandyfaelog Church (SA17 5PR), on the A484 from Carmarthen to Kidwelly; there is a memorial tablet to him in the church.

On his death the chapel was sold to the Methodists; the present building dates from 1813. One of the preachers associated with the church was David Charles (1762–1834), the brother of Thomas Charles of Bala. The ablest theologian of the Calvinistic Methodists in his day, he took part in drawing up their 1823 *Confession of Faith*. He and his son – also David Charles (1803–80) – wrote some of the best-known Welsh hymns. David Charles the elder owned a rope-making factory, and according to one tradition his majestic hymn extolling God's sovereign rule over all things, translated as 'Great Providence of Heaven', was written the day after his factory was completely burnt down. Another of his translated hymns is 'From

Griffith Jones' circulating schools

Griffith Jones is celebrated as the father of popular education and literacy in Wales. The spiritual ignorance of his flock grieved him, and he began to organize schools locally. Eventually, through his connections with the Society for Promoting Christian Knowledge (SPCK), they spread throughout Wales. A period of 3-4 months was considered sufficient to teach the pupils to read; the teacher – trained at Llanddowror – would then move on to a new district. Schools would be held both during the day and in the evenings; children and adults attended, and the tuition was free. All the accompanying literature was written and published by Jones himself.

By 1761 he had organized and funded over 3,300 schools, with the total number of pupils probably over 200,000. Through his untiring efforts it seems likely that almost half the population learnt to read the Bible; Wales thus became one of the most literate nations in the modern world. His main aim, however, was the spiritual well-being of his people. By teaching people to read the Bible he helped to prepare the way for the evangelical revival. He appointed many of the early Methodists as his schoolmasters – even though this exposed him to severe criticism within the Church of England – and there were close links between the schools and the early Methodist societies.

heavenly Jerusalem's towers'. His grave is in Llangunnor Church cemetery (SA31 2HY), to the east of Carmarthen, with delightful views of the Tywi valley.

In September 1979 Martyn Lloyd-Jones preached for the last time at Water Street. This was his 51st consecutive annual preaching visit to the chapel.

Llanddowror

Griffith Jones (1684–1761) came here as vicar in 1716. He was already a famous preacher, and known also for the appearances he had had to make before his bishop for preaching in the open air and other 'irregularities'. It was through his preaching in the winter of 1734-35 that Daniel Rowland was awakened to see his spiritual need. Jones gave

much counsel and support to figures in the emerging Methodist movement. However, he is mainly remembered for establishing a remarkable network of Welsh circulating schools with the aim of teaching people to read the

Above: *Bethany Calvinistic Methodist/Presbyterian Church of Wales Chapel, Ammanford*

Above: *The Old Theological College, Carmarthen (now the home of Carmarthen Evangelical Church)*

Bible in Welsh and learn the Church catechism. He and his wife are buried in Llanddowror Church, and a tablet on the wall commemorates him.

Llanddowror is just west of St Clears, towards Pembroke. St Teilo's Church (SA33 4HH) is in the middle of the village.

Pen-y-groes

Daniel P Williams (1882–1947) and W Jones Williams were brothers converted in the 1904 Revival. In 1913, having been introduced to Pentecostalism, they established a branch of the Apostolic Faith Church in the mining village of Pen-y-groes. In 1914, Daniel (or 'Pastor Dan' as he was generally known) was ordained in London as 'apostle' over the Welsh Apostolic congregations. W Jones Williams became a 'prophet' of the movement. In 1916 the Welsh congregations broke away to form the Apostolic Church in Wales which, with the addition of other Apostolic organizations in 1922, became the present world-wide Apostolic Church. The movement knew remarkable growth, particularly in Africa: there are about 4 million members world-wide and some 110 churches in Britain. From 1916 onwards an annual August convention was held at Pen-y-groes; it has now moved to Swansea. 'The Temple', the church building, is in Bryncwar Road (SA14 7PG) with Pastor Dan's grave outside.

For Pen-y-groes, take the A483 from Ammanford towards Llandeilo. At Llandybie Square turn left onto the B4556.

NORTHERN CARMARTHENSHIRE

It is remarkable that in four locations in rural north Carmarthenshire, all within a radius of some 10 miles (16 km) of the village of Llanwrda, lived four of the best known Welsh hymn-writers, all born within a period of 48 years (three of them within 19 years). Another hymn-writer, Ioan Thomas – usually associated with Llandrindod and Rhayader – was a native of nearby Myddfai.

Crug-y-bar

Dafydd Jones (1711–77) was a drover. Born in Cwm-gogerddan Farm, Caeo (SA19 8TR), he was converted while attending a service at the historic Troedrhiwdalar Chapel, between Beulah and Llanafan Fawr in Breconshire, on his way back from taking cattle to London. He joined the Independent Chapel at Crug-y-bar (SA19 8TH) and was a member there for the rest of his life. His first works were translations of Isaac Watts' psalms and hymns, and he afterwards published three volumes of original hymns. He is buried within the chapel walls, 'between the big seat under the pulpit and the doors'; there is nothing to indicate the grave, but in the cemetery there is a Welsh memorial to him on the prominent gravestone of Nansi Jones, a member of the congregation known as the 'Miriam and Deborah of the old Welsh revivals'.

Cwm-gogerddan Farm stands on the left on a minor road running eastwards out of Crug-y-bar and about a mile and a half from the village, which is on the B4302 between Lampeter and Llandeilo.

Above: *Water Street Calvinistic Methodist Chapel in 1813*

Above: St Teilo's Church,
Llanddowror

Llanfynydd

Born in the cottage of Efail Fach,
Cil-y-cwm, Morgan Rhys (1716–
79) was the most accomplished
of the first three. He was one of
the schoolmasters appointed by
Griffith Jones, Llanddowror,
for his circulating schools,
and taught in various places in
Carmarthenshire. He published
eight volumes of hymns between
1755 and 1774 with titles such
as 'Golwg ar Ddinas Noddfa'
('A View of the City of Refuge'),
'Griddfannau'r Credadyn' ('The
Believer's Groans'). 'His hymns
are characterized by profound
spiritual experience and he always
gives a prominent place to the
person of Christ' (*Dictionary of
Welsh Biography*). He is buried
in Llanfynydd churchyard (SA32
7TQ), in the hills to the north of
the A40 between Carmarthen and
Llandeilo.

Talley/Talyllychau

Thomas Lewis (1759–1842)
was born in Llanwrda, but
spent his life as a blacksmith in
Talley/*Talyllychau*, between
Lampeter and Llandeilo. The
walls of his blacksmith's shop
and stables (SA19 7YL) still
stand at the roadside in the
middle of the village. One of
the leading Methodist elders of
Carmarthenshire, he is unique
among Welsh hymn-writers in
being known solely for one hymn
– and that hymn consisting of
only one verse! Full of powerful
imagery drawn in part from
the smithy itself, 'Wrth gofio'i
riddfannau'n yr ardd' (translated
below) has been sung at
innumerable Communion services
in Wales over the years:

*The thought of Gethsemane's
groans,
The sweat on his body as blood,
His back ploughed by whips to the
bones,
The blows of his own Father's
sword;
To Calvary's hill led in pain,
And willingly nailed there for sin;
What tongue can in silence
remain?
What heart not be melted within?*

Thomas Lewis is buried in
St Michael's churchyard (SA19
7AX), which lies alongside the
12th century ruins of Talley
Abbey, one of the most tranquil
places in Wales. Behind the
church stands a yew tree; to the
left of both runs a path, and a few
plots beyond the tree, on the left
edge of the path, lies his grave. It
is now difficult to decipher the
wording on the gravestone, but in
front of it is a small memorial urn
bearing the inscription 'T. L.' and
the picture of an anvil.

Pantycelyn

Though these three – Dafydd Jones, Morgan Rhys and Thomas Lewis – were great Welsh hymn-writers, they were not the greatest. Nor would they have claimed to be so, for preceding them and known to them all was the work of 'the Sweet Singer of Wales' – William Williams of Pantycelyn (1717–91).

Above: Thomas Lewis' smithy and stables, Talley

Top: Cwm-gogerddan, home of Dafydd Jones

The founding fathers of Welsh Methodism will always be held in honour by Welsh Christians, though their names survive only in history books and on a few historical monuments. But the name and influence of William Williams are real and fresh to this day, and will remain so for as long as his hymns are sung.

Daniel Rowland and Howel Harris, with their almost unbelievable courage and the devastating power of the Spirit accompanying their ministries, formed the vanguard of the movement, but its genius was William Williams. It was his

The hymns of William Williams

For many Welsh-speaking Christians these form the life-blood of their spiritual experience. They provide an inexhaustible theological commentary and a rich source of encouragement, consolation, and stimulus to worship. Their predominant theme is the glory and excellence of Jesus Christ and his love. Williams stressed that their aim should be that 'Jesus alone should be exalted and that horrible little word "I" removed from them'. They are characterized by beauty and intensity of expression, plentiful colloquial and idiomatic phrases, fresh and sometimes startling metaphors, variety of metres and rhythms, and above all by the warmth and depth of the language that they provide for sinners to address their Saviour. The *Calvinistic and Wesleyan Methodist Hymn Book* of 1927 has 770 hymns, 247 of which are by William Williams. The 20th century hymnbooks of all the other Welsh denominations are not far behind in their acknowledgement of his superiority as a hymn-writer.

The great majority of his hymns were written in Welsh. The best-known of his hymns in English is 'Guide me, O Thou great Jehovah', which was partly translated by Williams himself. The following hymn, translated by Bobi Jones, demonstrates Williams' lively awareness of the vital relevance of biblical truth to himself and every believer:

In Eden – sad indeed that day –
My countless blessings fled away,
My crown fell in disgrace.
But on victorious Calvary
That crown was won again for me –
My life shall all be praise.

Faith, see the place, and see the tree
Where heaven's Prince, instead of me,
Was nailed to bear my shame.
Bruised was the dragon by the Son,
Though two had wounds, there conquered One –
And Jesus was His Name.

Above: *William Williams' grave at Llanfair-ar-y-bryn, Llandovery. (drawing by Rhiain Davies)*

Top: *William Williams and Pantycelyn Farm*

Above: *Evan Phillips*

theology and his incomparable understanding of the human heart – both of which were expressed so vividly in his literary works, his mastery of the *'seiat'* (the society or experience meeting), and especially his hymns – that left their indelible mark on the movement and ensured that its initial freshness, life, spirituality, and doctrine were maintained and nourished.

Pantycelyn is a working farm, owned by direct descendants of the hymn-writer. Williams was born at Cefn-coed Farm, less than a mile (1.6 km) to the north, but came to live at Pantycelyn, his mother's old home, when he married in 1748. The house contains many mementos of William Williams and the family are very welcoming to visitors. For more than two centuries it has without doubt been the most visited private house in Wales.

Almost 2 miles (3.2 km) from Llandovery on the A40 towards Brecon, turn left to the hamlet of Pentre-tŷ-gwyn. Pantycelyn (SA20 0RN) is on the right, a short distance further on.

Llandovery/Llanymddyfri

At one time the lively centre of the Welsh cattle trade, closely associated with the drovers who drove their herds to market in England, Llandovery also has important links with renowned figures in Welsh Christianity.

The William Williams Memorial Church (SA20 0PU), built in 1888, is the home of the English Presbyterian Church here. The pulpit has five carved panels with the central panel showing Williams writing a hymn. There is also a window commemorating the Montgomeryshire hymn-writer, Ann Griffiths (1776–1805).

Williams was buried at St Mary's Church, Llanfair-ar-y-bryn (SA20 0YF) on the northern outskirts of Llandovery. So great a gathering was expected at his funeral that over 500 pounds of cake was prepared for the wake. The church also contains a divided stained glass window: half shows Williams holding a harp of gold; the other half depicts Vicar Prichard with his 'Candle'. The grave cannot be missed in the small cemetery; nearby is the grave of his son, John Williams (1754–1828), principal of the Countess of Huntingdon's College at Trefeca 1786–91.

St Mary's Church lies to the left of the A483 as it leaves Llandovery towards Builth. A narrow road immediately after the hospital on the left leads to the church. Llandovery is also closely associated with Rhys Prichard (1579?–1644), often known as 'Vicar Prichard' or 'The Old Vicar'. He was probably born in the town and served as vicar here from 1602 onwards. He is renowned as the author of some thousands of simple Welsh verses, published posthumously by Stephen Hughes as *Cannwyll y Cymry* ('The Candle of the Welsh'), with the aim of teaching biblical truths to his parishioners. He had no intention of sparing their feelings; rather, he warned them of the wrath to come, urged them to seek Jesus Christ as their Saviour, and instructed them how they should then live as Christians in the light of Scripture.

'*Mene Tecel,*' O Llandovery!
God has weighed you in your misery;
Nought but dross in you he found,
Now beware his wrath profound!

Below: *Sunnyside, Newcastle Emlyn. The two cottages were originally one house*

In sinful man there is no trace
Of goodness to deserve God's
grace;
But in his goodness our God gave
His Son to seek, to find, to save.

Sell all your land, sell all your
gear,
Sell all your shirts, don't hold
them dear,
Sell all the good you can afford –
But never live without God's
Word.

There is a modern plaque
commemorating him in
Llandingad (or Llandingat)
Church, at the western end of
Llandovery. Erected on the site of
his old home, the Rhys Prichard
Memorial Hall stands by the
turning for Myddfai, just beyond
the William Williams Memorial
Church in the centre of the town.
His parents' house – and his own
birthplace – may well have been
what is now 33 High Street, a
short distance further along the
main road.

Newcastle Emlyn/
Castellnewydd Emlyn

In the middle of the attractive
little town of Newcastle Emlyn
stands 'Sunnyside' (SA38 9BN),
a dwelling that has particular
significance. Evan Phillips
(1829–1912) lived here from 1860
onwards. The minister of Bethel
Calvinistic Methodist Chapel, he
is notable for being one of the very
few men prominent in both the
1859 and the 1904 Revivals. It was
his itinerant preaching and that
of Dafydd Morgan that took the
1859 Revival to north Wales.

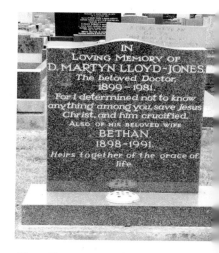

Above: *The gravestone of Dr and Mrs*
Martyn Lloyd-Jones

Tom Phillips, the pastor's
elder son, became an eye surgeon
in London, and his daughter,
Bethan Phillips, married Martyn
Lloyd-Jones in 1927. Dr Lloyd-
Jones's funeral service was
held in Newcastle Emlyn on 6
March 1981 at Bethel Chapel,
his grandfather-in-law's church
(SA38 9AB). The building is now a
chapel of rest.

Sunnyside is located near the
junction where the A484 from
Carmarthen enters Newcastle
Emlyn. The grave of Dr and Mrs
Lloyd-Jones lies in the town
cemetery, on the left a short
distance along the A484 towards
Cardigan. The grave is in the 7th
row to the left of the entrance,
near the top of the row.

⑧ Pembrokeshire and Cardiganshire
Light in the west

These neighbouring counties are somewhat different in landscape and language, but they have in common a beautiful coastline, an abundance of attractive beaches, and a long and blessed experience of the radiant light of the gospel

PEMBROKESHIRE/SIR BENFRO

Bosherston

The tiny St Govan's Chapel, wedged in the cliffs above the sea, probably dates from the 13th century but may have 6th century origins. Nothing is known of Govan with any certainty, but the chapel deserves a visit simply because of its stunning location.

Take the lane from Bosherston (SA71 5DP) across the firing range; access is restricted when firing is in progress! After a mile there is a car park; a set of over 50 steps leads down to the chapel.

Haverfordwest/Hwlffordd
Haverfordwest owes its long and prosperous history to its location at the lowest crossing point and highest navigable point of the Western Cleddau river. This history is rich in Christian associations.

At the junction of High Street and Dark Street, for example, a column (SA61 2DA) commemorates the spot where William Nichol, the third of the Welsh martyrs under Queen Mary, was burnt at the stake in 1558. According to John Foxe, he was 'an honest good simple poore man who was apprehended by the champions of the Pope for speaking certayn wordes agaynst the cruell Kingdom of Antichrist.'

At the top of High Street is St Mary's Church (SA61 2DJ). On the wall to the right of the altar is the gravestone of Sir John Philipps (1666?–1737), son of Sir Erasmus Philipps (d 1697) of nearby Picton Castle. Sir Erasmus was one of the deputies appointed by Cromwell to administer the important Act for the Better Propagation and Preaching of the Gospel in Wales (1650), which – despite the Acts of Union of 1536 and 1542–43 – acknowledged Wales as a separate entity by giving it religious self-government for three years. He also supported the Welsh Trust,

Facing page: The Pembrokeshire coast from St Govan's Head

set up by Thomas Gouge to improve religious and educational provision in Wales. With the help of Stephen Hughes and Charles Edwards, he published an edition of the 1588 Welsh Bible in 1677, distributing 1,000 copies to the poor.

Sir John, his son, was MP for Pembrokeshire and an uncle-in-law to the Prime Minister, Sir Robert Walpole. He donated much of his considerable fortune to the work of the Society for the Propagation of Christian Knowledge (SPCK) and the Society for the Propagation of the Gospel (SPG). In 1716 he presented the living of Llanddowror to Griffith Jones and for the last six years of his life was the sole financial support behind Jones' circulating schools. Jones married Margaret, Sir John's sister. During the illness and blindness of his last months, Sir John promised £30 to a young man to help him lead a movement lately set up in Oxford. That movement was the Holy Club, and the young man was George Whitefield.

Across the High Street from St Mary's is the entrance to Market Street, leading to St Thomas Green. At the corner of these two streets stands a block of flats, Moravian Court – a name of some significance in the history of the Evangelical Revival in Wales. On its wall a plaque notes that this was the site of the chapel and manse of the Moravian Church, the *Unitas Fratrum*. The chapel was built in 1773 and demolished in 1961. The story begins with the birth in Haverfordwest of William Holland (1711–1761), who went to work as a house-painter in London and attended the religious society at Fetter Lane. He was converted while introducing and reading Luther's *Commentary on Galatians* to Charles Wesley. This was the stimulus which led to the younger Wesley's conversion also. Then, seven days later, it was almost certainly Holland who read Luther's preface on *Romans* to the society at Aldersgate Street on the famous occasion when John Wesley was converted, his heart 'strangely warmed'.

Another Pembrokeshire man influenced at Fetter Lane by Count von Zinzendorf, the leader of the Moravians, was John Gambold (1711–71), who became a bishop of the Moravian Church in 1753. In 1763, his brother George established at Haverfordwest the only Welsh Moravian church. Because of ill-health, John returned home and looked after this flock until his death. The small garden of the present flats was the site of the church's graveyard; a plaque notes John Gambold's grave.

Following High Street to the pedestrian precinct by the

Above: *St Govan's Chapel, Bosherston*

river leads to 'The Old Bridge' over the Cleddau – built by Sir John Philipps in 1726 – and to the Prendergast district and St David's Church (SA61 2PJ). In the cemetery is the trilingual gravestone – Latin, English, and Welsh – of Howel Davies (c 1716–70), another of the first four 'fathers' of Welsh Calvinistic Methodism. Known as 'The Apostle of Pembrokeshire', he was converted through the preaching of Howel Harris and served as curate under Griffith Jones, Llanddowror. In his earlier days he itinerated throughout Wales and often occupied Whitefield's pulpit in Moorfields Tabernacle, London. Later he confined his ministry to Pembrokeshire and supervised a society membership of over 7,000.

Llwyn-gwair and Nevern/ Nanhyfer

Llwyn-gwair Manor (SA42 0LX), now a hotel and caravan park, was in the 18th century the home of the Bowen family. George Bowen (1722–1834) was a true friend to the Methodists, providing hospitality on their itinerant preaching tours and ensuring protection for them as an important member of the gentry. There are many references to 'Llanguire' or 'Llyngwair' mansion in John Wesley's *Journals*, as he stayed here while awaiting the tide that would take him to Ireland.

George Bowen appointed an 18 year-old Methodist as tutor to his children. The eldest daughter, Anne, fell in love with him; they married, and the tutor, David

Above: Llwyn-gwair, near Newport

Top: Memorial to Sir John Philipps, St Mary's Church, Haverfordwest

Griffiths (1756–1834), was given the nearby living of St Brynach's Church, Nevern. This was no case of mere nepotism, for 'Griffiths, Nevern' became one of the most powerful and convicting preachers in Wales. He was one of the few Welsh clergy chosen by the Countess of Huntingdon to serve in the chapels she established in London. He left the Methodists, however, the day after their separation from the Established Church in 1811,

R T Jenkins, the Welsh historian, wrote of David (d 589?), the patron saint of Wales: 'We know very little of St David. It is true that we are no worse off in this than our friends from Scotland or England. We know very little of Andrew, but at least we know that he was not a Scot. Less still do we know about George: in that we do not know at all who he was, it is not even worth asking whether he was English! But it is certain that David lived in Wales and that he was at least a quarter Welsh.'

According to one tradition David studied at Illtud's school in Llantwit Major. Although many of the stories associated with him may be discounted as myths, it is fairly certain that he was engaged in evangelistic preaching and that he opposed the heresy of Pelagianism which denied the sinfulness of human nature and a person's total dependence on the grace of God for salvation. His nickname, 'The Waterman', indicates the simplicity of his lifestyle. One source records his final exhortation as follows: 'Lords, brothers, and sisters, be joyful and keep your faith and belief, and do the little things that you have heard and seen in me.'

and his devastating sermons were heard no more in the quarterly and general assemblies.

Nevern Church is worth visiting for its bleeding yew, its remarkable late 10th or early 11th century Celtic cross, its Ogham stones, the memorial plaques to the Bowen and Griffiths families within the walls, and the Griffiths family graves outside.

Llwyn-gwair is on the left, about 1 mile (1.6 km) after Newport on the A487 towards Cardigan. The first left turn after Llwyn-gwair, onto the B4582, leads to Nevern.

Rhydwilym

Rhydwilym Chapel (between SA66 7QJ and SA66 7QH) is the mother-church of the Baptists of Carmarthenshire, and Cardiganshire. Its most significant feature is its position: secluded, far from any hamlet, exactly on the Pembrokeshire-Carmarthenshire border. The church was established in 1668 when Nonconformists were forbidden to worship in public; if officers of one county approached, the congregation could flee to the neighbouring county. In the first 170 years of its existence it planted eleven daughter-churches. The first building was erected in 1701.

Where the B4329 from Haverfordwest towards Cardigan meets the B4313 from Fishguard, turn right. At Maenclochog turn left for Llangolman. Just before Llangolman, a right turn downwards over the River Cleddau leads to Rhydwilym, on the Carmarthenshire bank.

St David's/Tyddewi

The impressive cathedral here is probably built on the site of David's settlement at Glyn Rhosyn (Latin: *Vallis Rosina*), in the area known as Mynyw (Latin: *Menevia*). The location offered convenient links with the Celtic lands of Ireland, Cornwall, and Brittany via the western seaways. The earliest part of the present building dates from the late 12th century.

The history of the shrine to David at the cathedral indicates the ebb and flow of theological tides. There was no shrine here from David's death until *c* 1100. In the medieval period a shrine was established, drawing pilgrims in their thousands; two pilgrimages here were equivalent to one to Rome! The Reformation swept it away in 1536, only for it to be rebuilt in 1920 and rededicated in 2012.

Above: *Nevern Cross*

The following individuals associated with the cathedral may be noted:

William Barlow, bishop 1536–1548. One of his actions as the first Protestant bishop was to remove the shrine to David.

Barlow's successor, Richard Ferrar, bishop 1548–1555, was martyred at Carmarthen.

The stories of Richard Davies (bishop 1561–1581) and Thomas Huet (precentor 1561–1565), the New Testament translators, belong to Abergwili, near Carmarthen.

Rhys Prichard, the 'Old Vicar' of Llandovery, was chancellor and canon here from 1626. Because the cathedral could not hold the crowds who came to hear him, he would preach in the open air. One tradition claims that he is buried in the cathedral churchyard.

William Laud (1573–1645) was bishop before his removal to Bath and Wells, and then to Canterbury. Fortunately for the local Puritans, he made only two visits to his cathedral during his five-year tenure.

David Howell, 'Llawdden' (1831–1903), was appointed dean in 1897. Much loved throughout Wales as a public lecturer and evangelistic preacher, he was buried within the cathedral walls, the first dean to be so honoured.

Woodstock/Wystog

On the B4329 from Haverfordwest towards Cardigan stands the famous Calvinistic Methodist Chapel at Woodstock (SA63 4TE), built in 1751 by Howel Davies (*c* 1716–70), 'the Apostle of Pembrokeshire'. His open-air congregations here often numbered many thousands. Soon after the chapel was built, George Whitefield passed through on a preaching tour and, on Davies' invitation, administered the Lord's Supper.

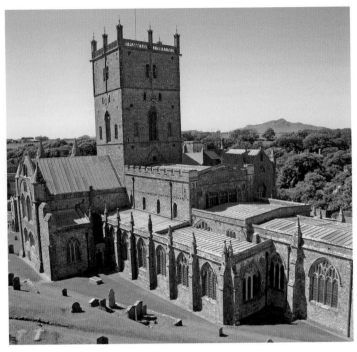

Above: *St David's Cathedral*

Howel Harris, however, condemned holding the service in a building not consecrated by a bishop. The incident reveals that Davies was more conscious of his independence from the Established Church than the other Welsh Methodists at the time. From 1751 onwards the Lord's Supper was celebrated regularly here, the chapel being emptied three or four times so that all might participate. It is still occasionally used for worship.

CARDIGANSHIRE/SIR ABERTEIFI (CEREDIGION)

Aberystwyth

'Aber' is not only a seaside town with marvellous views over Cardigan Bay but also the home of the nation's first university college and the National Library of Wales. Open to the public, the latter houses a superb range of printed books, periodicals, newspapers, manuscripts, maps, paintings, and photographs. Among its treasures are a copy of the first Welsh translation of the Bible (1588), the Calvinistic Methodist archives, Howel Harris's diaries, and the papers of Thomas Charles and Martyn Lloyd-Jones.

One of the main shopping areas is Great Darkgate Street. Halfway up, on the left-hand side above one of the shops, is a small Welsh plaque (SY23 1DE) commemorating the drawing up in 1823 of the Calvinistic Methodists' *Confession of Faith*, an excellent expression of biblical doctrine combined with spiritual warmth. The building was the home of Robert Davies, a grocer and an elder of the local cause.

Beyond the top of Great Darkgate Street and to the right stands St Michael's Church (SY23 2AU). The graveyard has been made into a parking area, lined by some of the old gravestones. Among them are those of Azariah Shadrach (1774–1844), who planted a number of Independent churches in the town and surrounding area, and Robert Davies. Another has the words 'Sacred to the memory of the late Venerable John Hughes, Archdeacon of Cardigan, Vicar of Llanbadarn Fawr'. One of the best-known Churchmen and preachers of his day, Hughes (1787–1860) actively opposed the sacramental high-church tendencies of the Oxford Movement. It was reckoned that there was hardly a house in Aberystwyth that he had not visited on some errand of mercy, and he was looked upon as a father to all, whatever their denomination.

In front of the Old College, facing the sea, stands a statue of Thomas Charles Edwards (1837–1900). The son of Lewis Edwards of Bala and great-grandson of Thomas Charles, he was converted during the 1859 Revival: 'Eternity pervaded the service, heaven was in the place . . . Before, I was a mass of damnation, and in the service I became a new creature.' When the first Welsh university college was established at Aberystwyth in 1872 he was appointed principal; he later succeeded his father as head of the theological college at Bala.

The present church at Llanbadarn Fawr (SY23 3QU), dating from the 13th century, stands on the site of the strategic centre for preaching and evangelism established by Padarn (c 560). It became a

Above: The National Library of Wales, Aberystwyth

centre of learning: Rhygyfarch wrote his *Buchedd Dewi* (The Life of David) here towards the end of the 11th century. William Morgan, the Bible translator, was vicar in the 1570s. In 1662 the vicar, David Jones (c 1630–1704), was ejected because of his Puritan convictions. He subsequently founded the congregation at Cilgwyn, near Llangybi, the first separatist cause in Cardiganshire and 'mother' of a number of other chapels. John Hughes served as vicar 1833–60.

for the deepening of spiritual life, and Seth Joshua's prayer, 'Bend us', greatly affected Evan Roberts (1878–1951), who was studying at Newcastle Emlyn for the ministry. During the 9 a.m. meeting Roberts fell to his knees praying, 'Bend me! Bend me! Bend us! Bend us!' The peace that flooded his soul and the sense of calling to speak to the young people of Moriah, Loughor (his home-town), drove him to begin his public ministry in early November 1904.

Blaenannerch

In front of the Calvinistic Methodist Chapel at Blaenannerch (SA43 2AL), on the A487 between Cardigan and Aberaeron, is the gravestone of John Jones (1807–75). Known as 'Old Blaenannerch', he was a powerful preacher who for over 40 years was the object of much esteem and affection in the Methodist assemblies.

In this chapel, on 29 September 1904, began one of those streams of blessing that eventually merged to become the 1904-05 Revival. Joseph Jenkins of Newquay and John Thickens of Aberaeron had organized a conference here

Capel Bangor

In front of Pen-llwyn Chapel (SY23 3LR), Capel Bangor, is a bust of Lewis Edwards (1809–87). Born in Pwllcenawon cottage on the opposite bank of the River Rheidol, he married Jane, granddaughter of Thomas Charles. He had to overcome opposition within the Calvinistic Methodists to a university education, but eventually studied at King's College, London, and under Thomas Chalmers at Edinburgh. On his return to Wales in 1837 he opened a theological academy at Bala, eventually becoming the elder statesman of the

Above: *'In this house was drawn up the 1823 Calvinistic Methodist Confession of Faith'*

Above: St Padarn's Church, Llanbadarn Fawr
Below: Bust of Lewis Edwards at Pen-llwyn, Capel Bangor

church, the main influence in 'presbyterianizing' it, and a major force in promoting an educated ministry.

Pen-llwyn Chapel is on the left as the A44 from Aberystwyth enters Capel Bangor. For Pwllcenawon (a private house on the site of the original building), turn right just before the chapel and then right again.

Llanddewibrefi

Llanddewibrefi was the scene of a dramatic sermon by St David, perhaps *c* 570, warning the assembled synod of the dangers of Pelagianism. His powerful preaching put a temporary stop to this heresy among Welsh Christians.

Sometime during the winter of 1734–35 Griffith Jones of Llanddowror preached at

CYFODWYD Y CERFLUN HWN I
ANFHYDEDDU COFFADWRIAETH
Y PARCH
LEWIS EDWARDS
M·A·   D·D·
SYLFAENYDD A·LLYWYDD·CYNTAF
ATHROFA'R BALA 1837-1887
A DYSCAWDWR CENEDL Y CYMRY

Llanddewibrefi (SY25 6RN). Aware of the mocking attitude of a young man, he stopped mid-sermon and prayed that God would send his Word into the man's heart. The prayer was answered, and from that day began Daniel Rowland's spiritual pilgrimage, although he remained 'under the law' and lacking in assurance for some time afterwards. His early ministry dwelt entirely on 'the terrors of law and of God'. In this state he sought the advice of Philip Pugh (1679–1760) of Cilgwyn, minister of a group of Nonconformist causes in central Cardiganshire. 'Preach the Gospel to the people, dear Sir, and apply the balm of Gilead, the blood of Christ, to their spiritual wounds, and show the necessity of faith in the crucified Saviour,' was the wise reply he received and acted on. Pugh's grave is in Llanddewibrefi churchyard.

Llangeitho

In December 2012 a plaque was unveiled on Albion House, Llangeitho (SY25 6TL), the shop – now also including a small café – that was the boyhood home of Martyn Lloyd-Jones. He attended the village primary school here, and aged ten was thrown to safety from an upper window when the house caught fire.

Although resident here for only ten years, Lloyd-Jones never forgot this period, not least because of the village's association with the greatest of all Welsh preachers, Daniel Rowland (1711–90). Although already an Anglican curate, Rowland was converted in 1735 through the preaching of Griffith Jones of Llanddowror. Because of the church's disapproval of his Methodism, however, he never received any preferment. Indeed, in 1763 he was deprived of his curacy at St Ceitho's Church, but his Methodist followers had built a meeting-house for him nearby – 'the New Chapel' – and he continued his powerful ministry there until his death. The fine statue of Rowland outside the chapel bears a Welsh quotation from one of his sermons: 'O Heaven! Heaven! Heaven! Your mansions would be much depleted if Zion did not nurture children for you on earth.'

Rowland's gravestone may be seen in the floor of St Ceitho's Church, 200 yards down the lane from the school. The 'New Chapel', or Capel Gwynfil, is in the centre of the village (SY25 6TW); much of the present building dates from 1861–63.

Above: *A plaque on Martyn Lloyd-Jones' home, Llangeitho*

In his early ministry Rowland would often preach on God's law, striking terror into hearts as he declared divine judgement on sin. In time, however, Christ's saving work on the cross was also given due prominence. Williams Pantycelyn's (translated) words vividly express Rowland's ministry:

Rowland's name was Boanerges,
Son of thunder, flaming, true,
Shaking heaven and earth together,
With a voice both strong and new;
'Come! Awake!' his voice in echo
Calls to all, 'our town's ablaze.
Flee this moment without turning;
God to ashes all will raze.'

He declared the law's strong terror
For some years with great alarm;
Many wounds were thus inflicted,
Then he sang with gospel charm;
He proclaimed divine salvation,
Full, complete, sufficient, free,
Through the death of the Messiah
Once for ever on the tree.

Translation by Eifion Evans in *Daniel Rowland and the Great Evangelical Awakening in Wales*, Banner of Truth, 1985.

On the monthly Communion Sundays crowds flocked to Llangeitho from all parts of Wales, often having walked through the Saturday night. They would retrace their footsteps on the Sunday night, reckoning that the sermons of the white-haired Elijah were ample reward for their efforts. Thomas Charles recorded his own experience as follows: 'January 20, 1773, I went to hear Mr Rowland preach at New Chapel. His text was Hebrews 4:15. A day much to be remembered by me as long as I live . . . I had such a view of Christ as our High Priest, of his love, compassion, power and all-sufficiency, as filled my soul with astonishment – with joy unspeakable and full of glory.'

Statue of Daniel Rowland, Llangeitho

Neuadd-lwyd

In 1810 Thomas Phillips (1772–1842), minister of the Independent Chapel in this hamlet (SA48 7RF), built a small schoolhouse to educate young men for the ministry. Over a period of 30 years, 200 ministers were trained here; such was the renown of 'Neuadd-lwyd Academy' that in 1831 Princeton Seminary awarded Phillips an honorary Doctorate in Divinity. His missionary zeal influenced many of his pupils – Thomas Jones went to Tahiti and Evan Davies to Penang – but the mission field that will be forever associated with tiny Neuadd-lwyd is that of Madagascar. David Jones (1797–1841) and Thomas Bevan (1796–1818) were local men, both aged 19, when they offered themselves as missionaries for Christ in Madagascar. After further preparation at David Bogue's college at Gosport, during which time they married, the party of six (each couple now having a baby a few months old) arrived in Madagascar in August 1818. Within three months all but David Jones had died from fever. He himself was at death's door, alone on an island of four million heathen and with the nearest Christian at Mauritius, some 450 miles away.

His story, together with those of David Griffiths and David Johns, both of whom studied at Neuadd-lwyd and later joined him, is that of the planting, persecution, and progress of the Christian church in Madagascar. Many native believers were killed and all missionaries were thrown off the island, but when they returned in 1867 they found some 50,000 believers – 'the blood of the martyrs is the seed of the Church'. A Welsh monument to Phillips and the missionaries outside Neuadd-lwyd Chapel includes the verse: 'Other sheep I have, them also I must bring.'

From Aberaeron take the A482 towards Lampeter; after 1.5 miles (2.4 km) turn right (sign: Derwen-gam). The chapel is a short distance up this minor road, on the left.

Rhydlewis

Outside St Michael's Church (SA38 9EX) at Troed-yr-aur, near Rhydlewis, stand the graves of the most eminent of father-and-son preachers in Wales. David Morris (1744–91), a great friend of Daniel Rowland, was considered second only to Rowland among the early Methodist preachers. In 1774 he became minister of nearby Twr-gwyn Chapel (SA44 5RY) – the first Welsh Calvinistic Methodist to be established as pastor over a single flock. The Welsh plaque on the chapel states that it was originally erected in 1750 for Rowland.

John Elias considered Ebenezer Morris (1769–1825), minister of Twr-gwyn after his father's death, to be the greatest preacher he had ever heard. He is particularly remembered for his attractive personality, but also showed courage in withstanding the authority and vested interests of the ordained clergy within Welsh Methodism after the days of the founding fathers. It was his forthrightness, together with the arguments of Thomas Jones of

Above: *Missionary Memorial at Neuadd-lwyd Independent Chapel*

Denbigh, that eventually brought Thomas Charles to agree to the break with the Established Church in 1811.

Just south of Tan-y-groes on the A487 from Cardigan towards Aberaeron, turn right along the B4333. At Beulah, turn left for Bron-gest, and in the middle of Bron-gest turn left (sign: Ffostrasol). St Michael's stands on the hill, on the left immediately before a crossroads; the large Welsh memorial column is on the left of the path to the church door. At the crossroads turn left for Rhydlewis, and left on entering the village. In the centre of Rhydlewis, turn right (sign: Pentregat). Just after the village hall, turn right up a steep lane. Tŵr-gwyn is towards the top of the lane, set back on the right.

***Above:** David Jones, Madagascar*

Tre-groes

Christmas Evans was born here in a cottage called Esgair-wen in 1766. There is a Welsh memorial plaque on the wall of the village school (SA44 4NN). A modern bungalow called Esgair-wen stands on the right a short distance beyond the school, near the site of the original cottage.

Take the A475 from Newcastle Emlyn towards Lampeter. A little beyond the Horeb crossroads, turn left at Gorrig for Tre-groes.

Tre'r-ddôl

Soar, or 'The Old Chapel', at Tre'r-ddôl (SY20 8PN) was until recently a museum commemorating Nonconformist life in Wales and the 1859 Revival in the locality in particular. The first leader of this revival was Humphrey Jones (1832–95), born in Tre'r-ddôl. Returning to Wales from America in 1858, he began to hold meetings at Soar, following Charles Finney's methods for 'creating' a revival: announcing 'revival meetings' beforehand, appointing an 'anxious seat' and fervently appealing to inquirers to come to the front. Within two months, however, his theology and preaching became increasingly unbalanced, and he eventually withdrew from public ministry. Thereafter Dafydd Morgan (1814–83) of Ysbyty Ystwyth was the main instrument used by the Holy Spirit to advance the revival throughout Wales. Soar is currently closed to visitors, but a plaque provides information on the significance of the site.

Turn off the A487 from Aberystwyth towards Machynlleth into Tre'r-ddôl; the chapel is at the far end of the village, on the right.

Wales yesterday, today, and tomorrow . . .

There have been times in Wales when, to quote the Puritan Walter Cradoc, 'the gospel has run over the mountains . . . as the fire in the thatch.' During the 6th century a 'llan' (church) was planted in virtually every part of Wales and the evangelical revivals of the 18th and 19th centuries had profound effects on the whole nation. Even in other periods the gospel flame continued to burn and it is almost possible to envisage the Christian faith folded among the contours of the beautiful Welsh landscape.

Today, things are very different. The spread of theological liberalism and the rejection of the divine authority of Scripture from the later 19th century rendered many churches and chapels impotent in the face of challenges from atheism, secularism, and materialism. There is widespread ignorance of the spiritual significance of many people and events named in this book. Some buildings and monuments referred to are dilapidated, while churches and chapels are closing at an alarming rate. The divine blessing experienced in Wales in the past makes the present decline all the more poignant.

However, it would be a mistake to conclude that the glory of the gospel has departed from Wales altogether. In addition to the faithful witness of many individuals, there are churches throughout the land – some with sizeable congregations – that stand for the same biblical truths embraced by so many mentioned in this book. Encouraging signs of spiritual life are also evident in recent developments in the older denominations, and in the work of numerous Christian organizations.

The thrilling evidence in Wales of God's remarkable activity in days past is an effective guard against despondency. Indeed, it provides encouragement to look to him to revive his work here again. And still more important, it is a powerful stimulus to worship.

Above: Plaque on Soar Chapel, Tre'r-ddôl, commemorating the 1859 Revival. It is based on 2 Chronicles 7:14: "The people humbled themselves. They sought the face of the Lord. God heard them from heaven and healed their land."

Acknowledgements

Copyright of pictorial material is gratefully acknowledged below; the material is included here by kind permission of the copyright holders. All other illustrations and photographs are either in the public domain or are copyright of the authors.

Page 6 Snowdon from Capel Curig © Dreamstime

Page 8 *Llanbadrig Church and Patrick's Island* © Tom Oates; Wikimedia Commons

Page 9 *An imagined picture of John Elias* © National Library of Wales

Page 13 *An imagined portrait of William Morgan by Thomas Prytherch* © National Library of Wales

Page 15 *Title page of the Welsh Bible, 1588* © National Library of Wales

Page 20 *Pistyll Rhaeadr, near Llanrhaeadr-ym-Mochnant,* © Velela: Wikimedia Commons

Page 32 *Philip Henry* © Mansfield College, University of Oxford; Wikimedia Commons

Page 34 *The attractive Gregynog Hall* © Gregynog

Page 46 *George Herbert* © Houghton Library, Harvard University. MS Eng 1405

Page 48 *Llyn Syfaddan/*Llangorse Lake, *near Trefeca, home of Howel Harris* © Dreamstime

Page 50 *Thomas Coke* © Oxford Brookes University; Oxford Centre for Methodism and Church History (Methodist Church House Collection)

Page 53 *Cefn-brith* © David Pike; www.daibach-welldigger.blogspot.co.uk

Page 59 *Cae-bach Independent Chapel* © Gerard Charmley; www.churches-uk-ireland.org.

Page 62 *Tintern Abbey* © Dreamstime

Page 71 *William Edwards* © Pontypridd Museum

Page 79 *Pontypridd Bridge* © Pontypridd Museum

Page 83 *Bethesda'r Fro Chapel* © Peter Wasp; Geograph Project, Wikimedia Commons

Page 90 *The upper Tywi valley* © Dreamstime

Page 94 *Title page of the first Welsh New Testament, 1567* © National Library of Wales

Page 98 *St Teilo's Church, Llanddowror* © David Dixon; Creative Commons

Page 110 *St David's Cathedral* © Dean and Chapter of St David's Cathedral

Page 111 *The National Library of Wales, Aberystwyth* © Ian Capper; Creative Commons.

	Christianity in Wales	*The Wider Context*
By AD 200	Christianity reaches Wales	
312		Constantine's 'conversion'
325		Council of Nicaea
382		Work begins on Latin Bible
By *c* 410		Roman armies leave Britain
5th century	Welsh Christianity revived from Gaul	Ireland evangelized
429	Garmon combats Pelagianism	
451		Council of Chalcedon
6th century	'Age of the Saints': Illtud, David etc	Earliest Welsh literature
c 563		Scotland evangelized
597		Augustine sent to England
664		Synod of Whitby
8th century		Offa's Dyke boundary built
1066		Norman conquest of England
1176		Eisteddfod at Cardigan
1282		Wales conquered by England
1384, 1396		'Wycliffe's Bible'
c 1390	Lollards active in Welsh Marches	
1400		Owain Glyndŵr's rebellion
1415		Martyrdom of John Huss
1485		Henry Tudor becomes king
1517		Luther's 95 theses
1534		Henry VIII rejects Pope
1535		Coverdale's English Bible
1536, 1543		Union of Wales and England
1555, 1558	Welsh Protestant martyrs	
1559		Calvin's *Institutes*
1567	New Testament in Welsh	
1588	William Morgan's Welsh Bible	
1593	John Penry executed	
1611		King James Bible
1620	Revised version of Welsh Bible	Pilgrim Fathers'
1621	Edmwnd Prys' Welsh psalter	
1630	The 'Little Bible' in Welsh	
1639	First 'gathered' church (Llanvaches)	
1642–48		Civil War

	Christianity in Wales	*The Wider Context*
1649	First Baptist church (Ilston)	
1650	Act for Propagation of Gospel in Wales	
1660		Restoration of monarchy
1662–89	Persecution of Nonconformists	
1678		Bunyan's *Pilgrim's Progress*
1681	Rhys Prichard's *Candle of the Welsh*	
1689		Act of Toleration
1731–32	Circulating schools begin	
1734		Jonathan Edwards: revival
1735	Conversion of Harris and Rowland	Conversion of Whitefield
1738	Conversion of Williams Pantycelyn	Conversion of Wesleys
1762–64	Llangeitho revival	
1768	College established at Trefeca	
1770	Peter Williams' *Bible*	
1793		William Carey goes to India
1800	John Davies goes to Tahiti	
1801–11	Thomas Charles' *Scriptural Dictionary*	
1804		Bible Society founded
1806	Ann Griffiths' hymns published	
1811	Welsh Calvinistic Methodists formed	
1817	Beddgelert revival	
1818	David Jones goes to Madagascar	
1841	Thomas Jones goes to Khasi Hills, India	
1855	Griffith John goes to China	
1859	Widespread revival	Darwin's *Origin of Species*
1872		Aberystwyth College founded
1887–88		Spurgeon: 'down-grade'
1891	Forward Movement founded	
1904–05	Widespread revival	
1920	Church of England disestablished	
1927	Martyn Lloyd-Jones at Aberavon	
1948	Origins of Evangelical Movement of Wales	
1985	Evangelical Theological College of Wales	
1988	*New Welsh Bible*	
1999		National Assembly for Wales
2004	Revised version, *New Welsh Bible*	

Welsh place names

aber   the mouth of a river. Often followed by the name of the river, e.g. Aberdyfi – the mouth of the River Dyfi.

afon   river

allt   hillside, wood

bach   small

bae   bay

banc   bank, hillock

bedd   grave

betws   house of prayer, chantry

blaen(au)   head, front, end, summit

bro   region, vale

bron   breast (of hill)

bryn   hill

bwlch   mountain pass

bychan   small

cae   field

caer   fort, castle

capel   chapel

carn, carnedd   cairn, heap, mound

carreg   stone

cas, castell   castle

cefn   ridge

cei   quay

celli (gelli)   grove

cil   covert, nook

cilfach   creek

clawdd   ditch, embankment

clogwyn   cliff, crag

coed   wood

coch   red

cors   bog

craig   rock

crib   ridge

croes   cross

crug   hillock, cairn

cwm   valley

dinas   city

dôl   meadow, dale

du   black

dŵr   water

dyffryn   valley

eglwys   church

esgair   ridge

ffin   boundary, edge

ffordd   road

ffos   ditch, dyke

ffynnon   well

glan   shore, bank

glas   blue

glyn   valley, glen

gwaun   meadow, moor

gwern   marsh, bog, alder-trees

gwyn   white

gwyrdd   green

hafod   summer dwelling

hen   old

hendre(f)   winter dwelling

hir   long

isaf   lower

llan   enclosed land where church erected. Often followed by the name of the associated Celtic saint, e.g. Llandeilo – the church of St. Teilo.

llwyn   grove, bush

llyn   lake

llys   court

mawr   large

maen   stone

maes   field, square

melin   mill

moel   bare (hilltop)

môr   sea

morfa   sea-marsh, fen

mynydd   mountain

nant   stream

newydd   new

ogof   cave

pant   valley, hollow

parc   field, park

pen   head, end, top

pentre(f)   village

plas   mansion, palace

pont   bridge

porth   port, harbour

pwll   pool

rhiw   hill

rhos   moor, plain

rhyd   ford

sain(t)/sant   saint

sarn	causeway	twˆr	tower
tal	front, end	tŷ	house
tir	land	uchaf	upper
tomen	mound, earthworks	ynys	island; river-meadow
traeth	beach	ystrad	flat land, vale
tre(f)	town		
troed	foot		

INDEX

People

SelectedTopics

* The Church in Wales came into being in 1920 as a disestablished member of the Anglican Communion, separate from the Church of England.

** In the 1930s the Welsh Calvinistic Methodists became known as the Presbyterian Church of Wales.